Networking for Every College Student and Graduate Testimonials

"As a recent graduate in both performing arts and administrative fields, I have learned that networking is not only beneficial in a job search—it is essential. The step-by-step instructions in this book not only inform recent graduates on smart networking approaches, but also enhance the outlook of working professionals, directing the reader on building and maintaining their personal branding and networking skills."

- **Michelle Puskas, professional dancer**

"I have been out of school for a while and working in the retail industry. My career was pretty satisfying and I had not thought about other career opportunities until I picked up a copy of '*Networking for Every College Student and Graduate*' and discovered some really interesting ideas which I decided to work on. Several months later, I have a whole new set of options. Great motivating book!"

- **Jeff Lunsford, retail store manager**

'*Networking for Every College Student and Graduate*' was a truly enlightening resource as a college student, and an even more transformational tool as a recent graduate. This book helped me position myself, brand, expand, and develop my professional network, and provided a strong foundation for the 'forever process' of networking."

- **Kristine Lester, Director of Community Outreach, DeVry University, New Jersey**

"It's true 'EVERYONE has an inherent talent to network' but we must choose to improve this necessary life skill. The practical insight to address your fears and easy-to-use tools to manage your contacts will benefit not just college students and graduates but anyone that wants to improve their quality of life."

- **Zarida Brokenborough, financial advisor**

"You are not just buying a book on business networking. You are buying a set of skills that will be with you for the rest of your life. After reading this book, business networking will come easily and naturally...everything you need to know about business networking. The art of business networking summed up into one book."

- **John Ciavttoni, computer network engineer**

Networking for Every College Student and Graduate

Second Edition

NETWORKING FOR EVERY COLLEGE STUDENT AND GRADUATE

Starting Your Career Off Right

Second Edition

Dr. Michael Lawrence Faulkner
Andrea R. Nierenberg

with a guest chapter
by Stephen L. Faulkner

Vice President, Publisher: Tim Moore
Associate Publisher and Director of Marketing: Amy Neidlinger
Development Editor: Russ Hall
Operations Specialist: Jodi Kemper
Cover Designer: Chuti Prasertsith
Managing Editor: Kristy Hart
Project Editor: Katie Matejka
Copy Editor: Chuck Hutchinson
Proofreader: Sarah Kearns
Indexer: Lisa Stumpf
Compositor: Nonie Ratcliff
Manufacturing Buyer: Dan Uhrig

Pearson offers excellent discounts on this book when ordered in quantity for bulk purchases or special sales. For more information, please contact U.S. Corporate and Government Sales, 1-800-382-3419, corpsales@pearsontechgroup.com. For sales outside the U.S., please contact International Sales at international@pearsoned.com.

Printed in the United States of America

First Printing October 2013

ISBN-10: 0-13-374113-3
ISBN-13: 978-0-13-374113-1

Pearson Education LTD.
Pearson Education Australia PTY, Limited.
Pearson Education Singapore, Pte. Ltd.
Pearson Education Asia, Ltd.
Pearson Education Canada, Ltd.
Pearson Educación de Mexico, S.A. de C.V.
Pearson Education—Japan
Pearson Education Malaysia, Pte. Ltd.

Library of Congress Control Number: 2013946778

To all of those college students and recent graduates who have made networking a tool of their success.

Table of Contents

Foreword

A day does not go by for me without someone reaching out as a colleague to receive information, to share information, to ask for or offer assistance, or just to provide an idea or suggestion. This form of communication is routine and nonthreatening, and therefore no one thinks twice about doing so. Yet the result of these conversations is the development of networks; I remember with whom I communicated and from whom I received sound advice, and they go on my list of folks to tap in the future on the topic. We develop formal and informal networks daily among coworkers, family, and friends without a second thought. Yet, when the expressed need arises to "network" for purposes of finding employment or extending our arena in a formal way, many begin to feel nervous and threatened, thinking it is "out of their league," particularly if they are facing this for the first time, as many new graduates may be doing.

Don't be fooled—young and old, experienced and inexperienced—all of us feel a certain trepidation at the thought of facing the public and "selling" ourselves. What if we are rejected? What if we don't somehow measure up? What if no one finds us worthy of being in their network? All of our fears come to the surface. I have known people who would rather have a root canal without Novocaine than face a room full of people they do not know and have to find some way to make conversation with them. I myself used to be one of those people who broke out in a cold sweat at the thought of an evening of "networking." Now I look forward to the times when I can get out of the office and interface with real people—and I never seem to find a topic I can't be conversant on.

What changed? I changed. Sometime ago, I realized that this was a fear I needed to overcome in order to be successful in the arena I wanted to thrive in.

So instead of turning down opportunities to network out of fear, I signed up for more of them and looked for opportunities to do so. Then I practiced some small techniques and made small progress each time until I felt comfortable walking up to a complete stranger and introducing myself, carrying on a conversation, and sharing a business card. Then an amazing thing happened: I actually began enjoying myself, began looking at these as opportunities to expand horizons and meet new people, many of whom were just as nervous at first as I was.

Don't discount the small opportunities that present themselves. I recently learned that the smallest amount of networking can yield unimaginable results years later. I began my career in the military and had a very interesting 11-year military career doing many things that my classmates would never have thought of doing. When I got out, I began to support a memorial project to honor the service of our military women.

Much networking is done to support charitable endeavors, and this project was no different. To support the project, a good 15 years earlier, I wrote a brief story about my military service. I submitted the story to the memorial and forgot about it.

Fast-forward to November 2009. To re-establish a tradition that had been conducted by First Lady Eleanor Roosevelt during World War II, First Lady Michelle Obama invited about a hundred service women and veterans to "tea" at the White House. I was honored to be invited. It was an amazing experience and probably one of the most daunting "networking" environments I had ever been in.

Can you imagine trying to "work the room" where military generals and high-level politicians were at every turn? But I hung in. Then the incredible happened.

While giving her welcome speech, Mrs. Obama quoted the story I had written 15 years prior. Had she not mentioned my name, I would not have even remembered what I had said that long ago. Not only was it an amazing and gratifying moment, but because the event and speech were broadcast on the Internet in a variety of ways, I received e-mails and communications from people—some from other countries— commenting on my quote and my service. I have established some wonderful new networks with some of them around our newly found common interests.

Michael Faulkner and Andrea Nierenberg have taken much of the guesswork out of the critically important process of networking for you by suggesting the "baby steps" you should take in each and every situation. As I read their book, I was reminded of many networking environments I had been in where their approach and the recommendations they make would have really made a difference. In essence, they have written the "how to" guide for the beginner networker, spelling out the many essential reasons for establishing a network as well as the reasons why so many feel uncomfortable doing so. They then provide page upon page of "baby steps" to building a solid networking approach and a comfort level that will bring great results. I only wish I had had this book with me at the White House!

Dr. Donna Loraine
Provost/Vice President of Academic Affairs for DeVry University

Acknowledgments

Thank you to Tim Moore, Publisher at Pearson Education, for his hands-on ability to make things happen and for his superior skills that have made many books like this very successful.

A huge thank you to all of the people at Pearson who contributed their amazing skills in pulling this book together.

Thank you to Russ Hall for his gift in writing and extraordinary editorial talents.

We are also so thankful to Frank Burrows of Pearson Learning Solutions for his belief in us and for introducing us to Sean Stowers, also of Pearson Learning Solutions, who thinks out of the box and was the one who networked us into the organization and opened the door.

And thank you to Linda Schuler for her administrative savvy and skills.

Thanks so much to all of you.

Dr. Michael Lawrence Faulkner and Andrea R. Nierenberg

About the Authors

Dr. Michael Lawrence Faulkner is a U.S. Marine Corps Vietnam veteran who served from 1964 to 1970 and rose to the rank of Staff Sergeant. He spent 30 years in a variety of leadership and management ("coaching") positions with Dun & Bradstreet, the Direct Marketing Association (DMA), and entrepreneurial start-ups, as well as helping run the family business before moving into the academic world. Today Michael is a professor at the Keller Graduate School of Management at DeVry University. Michael is a member of MENSA, a former two-time national champion of Athletic Dueling, and an International Rotary Fellowship award winner. He has been published in peer review journals, dozens of magazines, newsletters, Websites, and blogs, and has written half a dozen white papers, including one that was circulated to all elected members of Congress and the major media outlets. He has written or co-authored 11 books.

Andrea R. Nierenberg, best-selling author, speaker, and world-renowned business authority, is the force behind The Nierenberg Consulting Group. Called a "networking success story" by the *Wall Street Journal,* Andrea founded The Nierenberg Consulting Group in 1993. With a stellar 29 years as a leader in sales and marketing, Andrea is an in-demand business expert both at home and abroad. Her company partners with an array of the world's leading financial and media industry businesses.

Introduction

If you are like a lot of other college students or recent graduates, you've probably given the job market quite a bit of thought. It can be scary, right? Of course, there has been no shortage of advice from family members, friends, professors, and others. More advice you don't need.

This book is about experience and guidance in the most successful job searching and career building technique you can learn and use: networking. We have assembled years of successful observations, a great deal of research data, and the successful experiences of many individuals who have told us of their personal experiences with networking in lives.

Many people may feel awkward and shy with the process and techniques necessary to meet others and build a social network. The truth is, there are just as many other people feeling just as awkward and shy and hoping someone else will break the ice and start up a conversation. This book can help with information you need to take the first step.

We have put this information in guidelines, benchmarks, rules, steps, techniques, and various "how to" approaches to help you learn how to understand what networking is, how to develop your networking skills, how to build and develop your network, and how to use your networking skills in various situations.

We know that, without a doubt, networking is the single best way to help hundreds of thousands of college students, recent graduates, and our returning military hero veterans to enter or return to the workforce and get the job of their choice.

Reaching out with the suggestions, recommendations, guidelines, and step-by-step approaches outlined in this book should make it easier and more interesting.

Now, go out there and connect.

Michael Lawrence Faulkner

1

What Is Networking, and Is It Any Different for College Students Than Anyone Else?

Lawrence was nearing the end of his final semester and feeling pretty good about himself as he walked down the street that paralleled the campus. He was feeling good not just because he was about to launch out into the real world, but because he figured he pretty well had a leg up on the other students who were going to be fellow fish in the stream looking for those few choice jobs. He had lettered in tennis, done some summer theater, and had a wide circle of friends because he was one of the most outgoing members of his fraternity. He had five pretty good interviews lined up already.

Ahead he saw his former high school classmate Claire sitting at an outside table of the corner Starbucks. He hadn't seen her in a month or two. He couldn't resist. She'd been a top student back then, but she was about to find out how much good being a mousy introvert was going to do her at this stage of the game.

"Hey, Claire."

She looked up from a long list in her open notebook, brushed a long lock of brown hair away from her forehead. "Hey, back at you, Lawrence. All ready for the big job circus?"

She'd walked right into it. "Yep. I've got five interviews. How about you?"

"It depends."

"Depends on what?"

"How I can narrow down this list. I've got twenty-seven interviews, and that's narrowed down from thirty-five."

"Twenty seven?" He felt as though he'd just swallowed his gum, and he wasn't chewing any. "Are you kidding me?"

She saw him wobble on his feet and waved him to a chair across from her. She took a sip from her latte while he lowered to the wrought iron chair.

"The thing was," she said, "I got thinking about how many of us there would be going after the few really good jobs, so I thought I'd better get a jump on."

"But you were always so...shy. How did you do it?"

"Yeah, I knew I had some limitations, so that's why I started early to work around them. I may not always have to be so outgoing in whatever job I land, but I knew I had to do something different from all the other sheep that were just heading down the same old chute hoping for the best."

"What was it? What's your secret?"

"Networking."

"Still, that's so unlike you."

"Not really. It's just like when I knew I had to hone my study skills long ago and developed some best practices to get the most out of my time. There were steps, approaches, and before I knew it, I'm sorting through this pile of interviews."

Lawrence cleared his throat. "Is this...is this something anyone can learn?" He recognized for the first time a little humble eagerness in his tone.

"Sure," she said. "If you want to. I've got to say the dividends sure pay off."

* * *

Does the word "networking" scare you or, even worse, make you cringe? Are you fearful of what it might imply? Does the word imply that you might have to meet strange or different people or introduce yourself to people who might reject you? Or do you feel that networking is just some form of glad-handing or "sucking up" and that people who network get ahead because of "who they know, not what they know"? By the way, even if the myth "it's who you know, not what you know, that counts" were true, why would you ignore this pathway to success? Do you believe there is something inherently sinister, bad, or unfair about using contacts to help you get ahead?

Soon you will be given an opportunity to choose whether or not you will have the maximum control over your own pathways to life's success. You should be clear about one thing: You have not been chosen by some mysterious lottery or picked to appear on a new TV reality show or identified in any way as someone extra special. Although individually you are unique and special, just as everyone else is, everyone will have the same opportunity to make this choice at about the same time. Unfortunately, and this is where you begin to separate yourself, the vast majority of people will not recognize the moment of opportunity to choose and therefore will not get choices that you will. What separates you from them is that you are reading this book and opening your mind to the possibilities that await you.

This is one of the few moments in life when you will have the opportunity to experience near-perfect equality of opportunity for your own future.

Skeptics and doubters, those sheep-like people to whom Claire referred, prefer to live their lives in flocks of others like them, who dress alike, look alike, talk alike, work alike, think alike, act alike, believe alike, and like alike.

Perhaps you have heard the real statistics, seen the evidence, or even seen your friends' networking turn into opportunity after opportunity for them. Maybe you would like to network but feel that while you are in college, it may not be the "right" time, or maybe you feel that you don't have the experience, skills, or abilities to network properly. You may even have one of those ornery critters that appear every once in a while to sit on your shoulder (invisible, of course, to everyone but you) and criticize you unmercifully and try to convince you of how unworthy you are. That character will try to dissuade you from ever trying networking because you are not worthy. Now is the perfect time to put your fears and uneasiness to rest, to bury your concerns, to change your beliefs and ban that critter—that is, if you really want the greatest opportunities for success in life.

If you want the greatest chances for success in getting the jobs you desire and deserve; in meeting the people who are ready and willing to assist you in your aspirations; in being considered for the career opportunities you dream about; in getting the opportunity to be positioned for the best promotions; in getting the opportunity to be asked to serve on exciting committees and work with the most prestigious, influential, important people in the fields, industries, professions, and communities of your choice—if you want to have control of these choices, it is in your hands. It's your choice.

Of course, if you don't want any of these opportunities, or if you think getting them by having people help you would somehow diminish your character, stop here. There are others who will gladly take the help of people willing to assist them.

SELF-CONCEPT THEORY

Many psychologists speak of the Self-Concept Theory (SCT), which simply states that many of the successes and failures people have and will experience in their careers and lives are closely tied to the ways in which they have been accustomed to accept the view of themselves and their relationship with other people, including, of course, their parents, teachers, spouses, partners, bosses, managers, and supervisors.

You need to be aware of three critical points about SCT. First, the self-concept is learned; you are not born with it. You learn it by repeated experiences and your expectations of the outcome of those experiences, particularly with those in more powerful or influential roles, such as leaders, mentors, advisors, role models, and so on. Second, it is organized. You organize the feelings, beliefs, and world view of your self-concept because you generally desire order and harmony in your life. Last, the self-concept is dynamic, meaning you view the world not in isolation but in relation to your self-concept, which is subject to continuous re-evaluation as you attempt to assimilate new ideas and get rid of old ones.

Individuals attempt to maintain their self-concepts regardless of how helpful or damaging to themselves or others these self-concepts become. This truth is evidenced by individuals who often sacrifice physical and financial comfort, even their own safety, for emotional satisfaction to avoid change.

Individuals experience anxiety because of a loss of self-esteem, and anything that negatively impacts self-concept is a risk of depleting self-esteem. You can make SCT work for you or allow it to work against you. Most importantly, it is within your control. Some people accept this challenge; some people reject it. If you accept it, you exercise internal locus of control and are ready to make the choices to control your own life.

A great deal of research and empirical evidence prove something you probably know intuitively: Networking works for those who choose to work networking. It is, by an enormous margin, the single most effective technique for productive job hunting (even during economic recessions), career building, developing personal influence, solidifying leadership roles, strengthening effective management skills, developing personal communication skills, creating and improving organizational skills, learning how to work with individuals with diverse views, developing beliefs and skills, and generally enhancing the quality of your life.

The talent to network is inherent in nearly every individual. Almost anyone can learn how to network. However, the drive, energy, skills, ability, desire, and knowledge by which networking is learned and perfected can be mastered only by those who are willing to devote the belief, time, energy, and resources to doing it properly. Therefore, although most people instinctively know or can eventually figure out that networking "works"—which is why we get the myth "it's who you know that counts"—only a limited number of devoted individuals manage to reap the huge rewards of successful networking.

A study of UCLA graduates found that nearly 75 percent believed it was the people you knew that counted. What is interesting about this finding is that three-quarters of the graduates believed they knew the secret to success, yet they could not bring themselves to actually do what it took to become networkers. Furthermore, 70 percent of the replacement jobs were handled in the same manner. These jobs were not posted on any Web site, advertised on any classified page, listed with any headhunter or recruiter, or otherwise publicly posted. These jobs were filled by the hiring managers' use of their social networking. The hiring managers first looked at people they knew and trusted, and if that approach did not turn up the candidate they wanted, they asked their network—their own contacts, the people they knew and trusted (if they knew of any candidates they knew and trusted).

People already in the workforce who have learned to take advantage of the skills and benefits of networking will confirm that they get many more opportunities than their peers who do not network. Many college students are just not aware of the value and benefits of networking and therefore do not practice the skills; consequently, they do not take advantage of the benefits, leaving this enormous opportunity untapped.

In just one area—jobs—networking can mean the difference between jump-starting your career and spending years in unsatisfying, unfulfilling dead-end jobs.

There is some evidence by economists that unemployment will be a societal problem in America for years into the future. Networking could be the difference between being part of the pool of college graduates working in low-level unsatisfying jobs and those who move their careers along regardless of the state of economy.

Knowing how the hiring process really works is just half of the benefit of networking. The other half is knowing in advance what hiring managers really want in new hires. In a number of empirical research studies conducted over the past ten years, senior managers of a wide range of businesses were asked about what they were looking for in recent college graduates. The following is what they said they value most in the order of the most frequently cited skills, characteristics, and talents:

- Good communications skills

- Interpersonal skills

- Ability to find and fix problems

- Enthusiasm

- High energy level

- Strength of character

- Self-confidence

- Motivation

- Leadership skills

- Quick adaptability to change and uncertainty

- Good listening skills

- Commitment to lifetime learning

- Commitment to excellence

- Being a team player

- Willingness to take some risks

- Willingness to face self-assessment

- Ability to lighten up (to not take oneself too seriously)

In a survey conducted online in July 2009, 77 percent of the respondents indicated that they felt "soft" skills were more critical for new college graduates to possess. Of these respondents, 14 percent felt it was best for graduates to have good communications skills, 23 percent thought interpersonal skills (networking) were most important, and 40 percent felt the potential to learn or be taught was most critical. Nearly three-quarters of what respondents felt were the most important things for recent college graduates to have could be shown to employers only through face-to-face meetings or, more importantly, to networking contacts who then relay this information to other contacts.[1]

In a nationwide study conducted in 1999 by RHI Consulting, which provides information professionals to organizations, 27 percent of Chief Information Officers responding reported that strong interpersonal skills were the single most important quality in job candidates followed by technical skills, as cited by 23 percent of the respondents.[2]

In December 2006, Peter D. Hart Research Associates conducted a comprehensive study of employers and recent college graduates for the Association for American Colleges and Universities. The study found that a significant majority of respondents cited skills learned and perfected in networking as the most important skills employers look for in new hires. These skills and the percentage of respondents reporting them as the most important skills are shown in Figure 1-1. The skills are teamwork (44%), critical thinking (33%), and oral/written communications (30%).

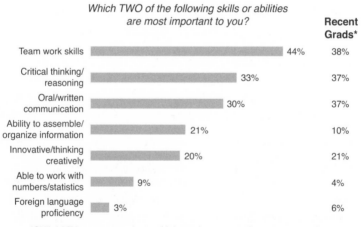

Most Important Skills Employers Look for in New Hires

Which TWO of the following skills or abilities are most important to you?

		Recent Grads*
Team work skills	44%	38%
Critical thinking/ reasoning	33%	37%
Oral/written communication	30%	37%
Ability to assemble/ organize information	21%	10%
Innovative/thinking creatively	20%	21%
Able to work with numbers/statistics	9%	4%
Foreign language proficiency	3%	6%

*Skills/abilities recent graduates think are the two most important to employers

Figure 1-1   The most important skills employers look for in new hires.

In a poll conducted in June 2009, Michael asked business managers, managers, and supervisors what they considered the most important skills or traits for recent college grads.[3] Table 1-1 shows how 293 respondents answered.

Table 1-1

Skill/Trait	Respondents (%)
Potential to learn/be trained	40
Interpersonal/team skills	23
Communication skills	13
Proven achievement/experience	12
Technical/technology knowledge	9

This poll reaffirms employers' high regard for the soft skills and talents—that is, ability to learn, ability to get along, and communication skills.

So, if the idea of networking scares you or puts you off, or if for some reason you think that because you are a student or you are young, networking isn't for you, you need to know something important:

- You are not alone. Believing you are alone may be a reason you have shied away from the very skill that can help you professionally and personally.

- You don't have to wait and try to learn the benefits and value of networking as you mature. Many college students felt that way before they learned the benefits and value of networking while in school.

The earlier you start, the sooner you will be proficient and the sooner you will start gaining the benefits of networking. This is the skill that can begin helping you right now while you are in school. You are never too young to begin networking.

Why You Need to Know How to Network Effectively

No one can predict or forecast success for every endeavor, but if you learned there is a success rate of nearly 60 to 70 percent for engaging in a particular behavior, wouldn't you want to learn as much about that behavior as possible? Well, prepare to alter your behavior and probably your beliefs. According to research conducted by Cornell University Career Services, 70–75 percent of all newly created jobs and replacement positions are never posted anywhere.[4] This means these jobs are never listed on the Internet; recruiters and headhunters don't know about them; they don't appear on Craigslist, MySpace, or Monster.com; and the respective human resources departments may not even be aware in advance. The people who know about the open positions are the hiring managers and their networks.

One of the fundamental credos of both networking and human nature is people are nesters and prefer to be around and work with other people whom they know and like. This is not a mystery of the universe or a great discovery of science; it is simply human nature. Even wolves seek out others like themselves for their small but family-like packs. Given the opportunity, hiring managers will first attempt to hire people they know and like. Think about it, and it will make sense.

A manager spends about eight to ten hours a day with an employee; there are probably hours spent in travel or social time, and the manager wants to know he or she is able to enjoy the time spent with the employee. In addition, the manager wants to be certain he or she can trust the employee.

Trust and reciprocity are traits and talents people bring with them to the job that can't be taught. Managers can teach new employees the job requirements; they can't teach new employees to get along with others, to unilaterally find and fix problems, to have good interpersonal skills, to be adaptable to change or uncertainty, or to be willing to take risks. These kinds of traits and talents are found in people whom managers find from their own networks. If hiring managers cannot find someone they know and like, they will extend their personal network of contacts and ask others whom they know and like if they know anyone who could fill the position. People put great stock and trust in their contacts' networks. If their contacts know and like someone, that candidate has (unbeknownst to him or her) already made a great first impression on the hiring manager.

If hiring managers cannot find candidates whom they know, or a network contact knows, the traditional job hunting approaches and tools are put to work searching for prospects first with "experience," those who, hopefully, will become people the hiring manager will come to know and like. Lastly, if no one with experience is available, prospects with "potential," which usually is the code word for recent college graduates or college students about to graduate, are interviewed.

Even if the word "networking" does make you cringe, you should at least be aware that you need to develop this skill to be successful. Don't buy into the myth that there is something wrong with the expression "It's not what you know but who you know." This old saying is truer than ever in today's competitive world.

Most often, the "who you know" does not necessarily lead you to the next job or the next new client or the funding for your new business or the successful new project in your company or whatever you may be looking for in life, professionally or personally. Rather, it leads to the opportunity to be in the position to be considered for the job, to meet the potential new client, to have a favorable introduction and positive meeting with funders, to be favorably considered above others for a new project, or to have any number of professional or personal opportunities presented to you that others will not get.

Networking is not a tool by which you should expect to be handed gifts that you are not qualified for or given responsibilities you are not capable of handling. "Who you know" is hardly ever enough in itself to get someone anything (unless you have the same last name and DNA of the other person). What you want from networking is the inside track, the most favored treatment, the full and undivided attention of the decision maker or influencer to make your case. This, of course, is something that the other candidates almost never get.

The Gallup organization has done extensive research in what employers look for, and firms repeatedly claim they want four things:

1. Skills

2. Knowledge

3. Experience

4. Talents

The skills that managers want are the soft skills we already mentioned such as communications skills, interpersonal skills, the ability to find and fix problems, and a work ethic. These skills are developed and reinforced in networking experiences.

The knowledge component consists of a job applicant's intelligence. The experience issue is not a critical matter if the hiring manager is already sold on the applicant's intelligence and skill level. An intelligent applicant can be taught most jobs.

The real issue is talents. Most firms are not good at assessing an individual's talents—an applicant's recurring patterns of thought, feelings, actions, and behaviors that naturally equip the individual to excel in a job. Therefore, the applicant, using networking and communications skills, has to take charge and be able to demonstrate his or her talents and how he or she will benefit the employer.[5]

What do applicants have to do?

- Demonstrate they will reduce the cost of the hire, lower the employee turnover rate, and improve interpersonal relationships with other employees.

- Demonstrate they are easy to manage, are quick to learn roles, adapt quickly to change, and therefore have a shorter learning curve.

- Demonstrate they will be more productive, more precise, and more consistent; will miss less work; will produce higher-quality work; will make fewer mistakes; will reduce management anxiety and stress; and will exceed expectations.

- Demonstrate they will produce greater customer satisfaction, greater customer retention, and higher profits.

To do all of this, you need time and the undivided attention of the decision maker. You need for the decision maker to start with a favorable opinion of you and allow you to build your case from there.

Andrea has a friend who is a great photographer. Her pictures really give true meaning to the phrase "a picture is worth a thousand words." She captures the essence of her subject in each photograph. Yet she puts off starting her own photography business. As she says, "I don't feel ready yet." Andrea believes her photographer friend is fearful of getting out there and building the relationships that will help her grow her business. In other words, she is scared of networking.

Andrea's friend the photographer knows all this. She is a well-educated, competent, professional woman. She has many contacts from her previous career as a marketing manager and knows the value of marketing oneself. Like many of us in the wake of current events such as the terrorist attacks of September 11, 2001, she wants very badly to achieve goals that have become even more important to her. She knows she has to overcome her resistance to networking, yet she can come up with a million and one excuses not to network.

In one of Michael's courses at DeVry University, he spends a great deal of time on the networking issue and has the students make a list of 25 people they know by first name.

From this list, the students pick a half-dozen contacts and make calls from the classroom, write letters, and seek to set up networking meetings with two to three contacts. In this step-by-step approach, Michael attempts to show that networking isn't something to be feared and that it is something everyone can do with a little effort. The experiences of many college students, recent graduates, and the photographer are fairly common. Do any of the following sound familiar to you?

- "I'm really a shy person."
- "I wouldn't know where to begin."
- "I am only a college [freshman, sophomore, junior, senior]. Who would be interested in networking with me?"
- "No one would be interested in me or what I have to say."

- "I tried making contacts (networking) once, and after three months, nothing happened, so I gave up."

- "I'm uncomfortable starting a conversation with a stranger."

- "I don't know how to keep a conversation going or how to gracefully break away when it's time to move on."

- "I'm embarrassed to ask someone for a favor."

- "I'm a private person. When I get on a plain or a train, the last thing I want to do is chat with the person next to me."

- "I'm busy. I hardly have enough time in my life for the people and activities I really care about—family, friends, my kids' soccer games and recitals, or taking a class."

- "I don't care for the type of people who call themselves 'networkers.' I think they are only interested in getting something from me."

- "I don't know how to keep track of my contacts. My address book is a mess, and I don't have a smart phone or the right software on my computer."

- "I haven't followed through with the contacts I've managed to make; therefore, when I do need more information or help, I'm reluctant to make the call."

- "I'm only a student, and a junior at that. I will have plenty of time to network late in my senior year."

- "I am just a student, and students don't have any opportunities to meet people who count or who are important."

- "With the technology degree I am getting, it is such a specialty I won't need much networking in my field."

- "As a student, I don't have that much work experience to tell people about."

We can relate to these feelings. We were both students. Networking has become easier the more we have done it, but it wasn't always easy. We were both very shy. When Andrea first moved to New York City, she knew no one except her grandparents, but today she has a database of more than 2,500 people, and it's still growing. She will tell you that she found out that networking was the one sure way she could enrich and empower herself early in her career.

Michael grew up painfully shy and self-conscious, using self-deprecating humor and athletics to cover for his low self-esteem. He has a learning disability, which he did not discover until he was an adult and had learned his own successful coping mechanisms through trial and error and facing many, many failures.

Andrea's basic theory on networking is this: "It is the opposite of not working. In other words, if you are not making connections, and nurturing the relationships you have developed, you are simply 'not working.'"

Why Networking Works: You Already Have the Resources You Need...You Just Have to Put Them to Work

The scientist John Milgram developed a theory called the "small world theory." Dr. Milgram's theory suggests that everyone in the world is separated from everyone else by just six contacts. Dr. Milgram did a series of famous experiments that proved his theory. This theory has not only been proven but strengthened by a more recent study in which e-mail was used. This experiment found we are separated by just 4.5 contacts. Furthermore, if you use the social Internet site LinkedIn, you can see how this is possible by the raw numbers of third-level contacts. The implication for networking is profound even if you were to actively network with only a tiny fraction of the potential you are capable of reaching. Each network contact you have is likely already networked, which, given the proper approach, care, and feeding, means your contacts should grow by some multiple.

The key phrase here is "the proper approach, care, and feeding." Your network is available for you to enrich your professional and personal life, but in return you must enrich the lives of others.

We get very upset when we hear someone say, "It's time to start looking for a job. I better start networking." Or "I only network at certain meetings or events." Networking is a skill, and like any personal skill, it needs to be practiced to be perfected.

You can't just sit down at a piano once a month and play Bach concertos like they are supposed to be played, nor can you network properly on occasion or on demand just whenever the need might arise. Networking really is a simple five-step process, but even though the process is simple to define, the work is hard. The following five-step process is available in Appendix A:

> **Step 1: Meet People.** You have to mix it up and get to know them. In Chapter 3, "Creating Connections: The People You Need in Your Network," you consider examples of "breaking the ice" introductory phrases that you can use or adapt for your own style.
>
> **Step 2: Listen and Learn.** People like to talk about themselves and/or their company. When you actively listen, you learn about what is important to them, who they are, how you could help them, and how they could help you. In Chapter 5, "When Networking Doesn't Come Easy: Networking for Introverts," you explore the difference between real empathetic listening (when you engage in active and responsive listening) and listening in which you are just "hearing" what was said.
>
> **Step 3: Make Connections.** Help people connect with others you know can help them.
>
> **Step 4: Follow Up.** Keep your promises; keep your word. If you promise to do something, do it in a timely manner. In Chapter 7, "Keeping Your Network Alive and Growing," you see an easy-to-use method for helping you follow up with contacts.
>
> **Step 5: Stay in Touch.** After an initial period of contact, if a result does not materialize, most people just move on. This is the point at which the Nierenberg System, which you will explore in detail, really works for successful networkers. These folks find ways to stay in touch and continue to build relationships. Why? Because their goal is to build a network of long-lasting, mutually beneficial relationships, not just to get an immediate "result." This five-step system works because it is based on building long-lasting relationships—those that are not just immediate, but lifelong.

"Networking" is one of the most overused and misunderstood words in common vocabulary today. When you hear the word, what comes to your mind?

- Getting something from someone else?

- Using others?

- Coercion?

- Manipulation?

- Getting something without using your real abilities?

- Having a "godfather" or mentor who will smooth the way for you even if you are not capable or qualified?

- Making hundreds of daily short digital contacts on social networking sites?

Or do the following descriptions come to mind?

- Deserved enrichment

- Empowerment and influence

- The chance to learn something new and help others get what they want

- An opportunity to meet interesting people

- The best method to achieve a professional or personal goal

- The real world—the way more than 60 percent of jobs are filled

- The way people prefer to select prime candidates for choice competitive opportunities

You need to deal with the negative and inaccurate impressions of networking right now. In some of the negative impressions we listed, some people express a dark side of networking. It really isn't even networking that is being discussed, but the dark side of human characteristics. Because some individuals abuse networking, others confuse that abuse with networking itself.

Networking is the most powerful tool individuals can use in their careers and lives. It should not come as any surprise that some people out there are not benevolent, gracious, nice, friendly, kind, fair, helpful individuals. Instead, you will find the occasional malevolent, malicious, spiteful, wicked, nasty, mean, power-hungry, self-centered, egotistical, narcissistic jerk.

These bad seeds can just as easily master the understanding of body language and fake networking techniques (fool some people for a short period of time) and/or use their genes, money, power (not influence), and even evil to get ahead.

Furthermore, people who advance solely on the coattails of a godfather or mentor are quickly seen as empty suits and frequently are abandoned or exiled, and they eventually will fail or wither away in ignominious insignificance. All these examples explain how networking gets an inaccurate and even a bad name.

What these evil people do is abuse power and employ treachery. They are not networking; they are power brokering or using power tactics instead of influence.

Networking is lifelong and beneficial to everyone who participates. It is a win-win proposition. Power brokering by its nature is a zero-sum political contest in which someone must win and someone must lose. In the long-run, an individual who practices power brokering creates a long list of enemies who will do anything they can to bring that person down. Unlike networkers, power brokers have few friends.

Real networkers gain the positive benefits listed earlier because they gain the help and assistance of an ever-growing number of people. If you are a little more technically minded, here is the actual formula for why networking is so successful if done properly.

There is a formula called Metcalfe's law, named for Bob Metcalfe, the founder of 3Com. The law, which was created for computer networks and was applied to the Ethernet, applies just as well to social networks. It says that every time you add one more user (contact) to a network, you add value not only to that user but to every other user already there and to any other user who eventually joins.

The classic example of how this system works is the telephone. One telephone (one network contact) has almost no utility value as a network. You can't call or contact or network with anyone else. However, the second telephone adds significant value to the first and the second because networking can now take place. The third, fourth, and so on add more and more value to all current telephones plus all new telephones (contacts) that are added.

Summary

We live in a very competitive world. Today it is never too early to learn the business and life skills that will give you the competitive edge when you graduate from college.

In the chapters ahead, you will explore the hands-on steps and processes to take you from college days to the world of business. You will learn that you may already be networking; you just may not call it that.

You will learn everything from creating connections to being aware of how each person you meet can be a potential connection whom you could help and who could possibly help you. You will learn how to become head and shoulders above every other college student—whether a freshman, senior, or recent graduate—in finding the job you want. You will learn how to get promoted and how to become a true business leader.

Endnotes

1. Michael Faulkner, My polls. LinkedIn. http://polls.linkedin.com/. Accessed June 30, 2010.

2. C. F. Gray and E. W. Larson. 2008. *Project Management: The Management Process*. 4th ed. New York: McGraw-Hill/Irwin.

3. Faulkner, My Polls.\ LinkedIn, July 2, 2009.

4. Cornell University Career Services. "Networking Events." http://www.career.cornell.edu/events/networking/

5. Gallup. 2009. Strengths-based development: Using strengths to accelerate performance. www.gallup.com/consulting/61/Strengths-Development.aspx. Accessed January 10, 2013.

2

Positioning Yourself and
Your Brand, "You"

Sarah Ann did pretty well getting registered, putting on her name tag, and moving down the hallway to where she could look through the doorway and see people milling about, chatting, and visiting a long refreshment table along one wall. Then her feet turned into lead and butterflies began to churn and whirl around inside her—big sumo wrestler-sized butterflies. This wasn't her thing at all.

A hostess just inside the door saw her pull up short, maybe saw her eyes widening. She smiled at Sarah Ann, waved a hand to come inside.

Sarah Ann took slow leaden steps inside the doorway.

"There you go," the hostess said. "Now get out there and mingle; get to know some people better."

The crowd looked harmless enough, some even smiling, but for a second or two she thought of sharks swimming in a pool.

You begin by beginning, Sarah Ann thought. Now, come on! She took a step, then another, and before she knew it she was talking to someone, trading business cards. Someone came up to her, she talked some more. This isn't so bad. She moved through the crowd, joined a small group briefly, and then talked with three different people one-by-one. Piece of cake. While moving along the refreshment table line, she even got into a conversation that introduced her to three more people and turned out to be one of the most productive moments of the evening.

Making that plunge had been the hardest part, but after she got rolling, she was plowing through the milling throng and making new friends and contacts left and right. Being prepared made all the difference. She had to tip her hat to those Boy Scouts, whose motto is: "Be prepared!" There was a lot to be said for that.

* * *

Maybe you would feel the same at first, in a similar situation, and wonder, "How do I begin?"

How would you have felt if you had been in Sarah Ann's place? Well, how do you feel in any situation such as before class, before a school event or activity, or at any gathering when you have 15 minutes to "network" before things get started? What are you thinking when you attend a "networking" event at a school social function, convention, business meeting, class, or seminar? What is your attitude when you join a school club, voluntary membership organization, professional society, trade group, or other special-interest group? Do any of the following thoughts run through your mind?

- How do I approach a classmate or peer or fellow delegate or business associate and introduce myself?

- Is it up to me to keep the conversation going? If so, how do I do that?

- What if I'm the only new person and everyone else already knows each other? Will they think I'm pushy or intruding?

- How do I break the ice? What is the best or safest thing to say?

- How do I break away from someone so I can keep on mingling?

- How long should the first networking encounter last?

- What if someone asks me a question for which I don't know the answer?

Don't fret. You are not alone. Many people who attend events, social activities, seminars, and workshops express these same feelings about networking. It's hard to break old habits.

When you are not familiar with the simple techniques of effective networking, you naturally tend to stay within your comfort zone. It is comfortable to hang out with our friends or to stand in the corner and wait for the meal or event to begin. Yes, even eating rubber chicken seems like a better option than talking to someone you don't know. However, this is not taking advantage of the opportunities at hand. Unless you are making new contacts all the time, your network is not growing.

Give Yourself Permission

You have to give yourself permission to network. Changing your attitude to a positive one is the first step to success. Just allowing yourself that "switch" in your mindset can make all the difference. Then you need some techniques you can immediately use when you walk into a room full of people or when someone announces, "It's time to network."

Fourteen Easy-to-Use Techniques for When "It's Time to Network"

Here are 14 easy-to-learn, easy-to-use techniques that you can use immediately to become an effective networker while you are a student. The following list of techniques is also available in Appendix B:

1. Have a business card.

2. Have an "ice breaker" opening line.

3. Develop your 20- to 30-second "branding statement." Some people call this an "elevator statement" because you should be able to complete it on a short elevator ride. This infomercial about yourself provides the listener with a reason to pay attention to you.

4. Do your research; know something about your potential network associates.

5. Have a list of "get to know you" questions prepared and practiced so you sound natural.

6. Develop a list of idea generator topics ("small talk").

7. Get in line.

8. Take a deep breath; visualize yourself engaged in a thoughtful, interesting, and memorable conversation; and dive into a group.

9. Look for a designated host or greeter, and start there.

10. If you and the contact have your hands free (no juggling of plates and glasses), extend your hand first and offer a firm (but not bone-crushing or limp) handshake and introduce yourself. Be sure to consciously talk slower than you normally would because your adrenalin is pumping and you'll be talking faster than you think.

11. If you are seated at a table, start a conversation with the person to your right or left.

12. Have an exit strategy, a "break the contact" comment that allows you both to break off conversation gracefully.

13. Set a goal for every event or activity you attend to build your network by some number.

14. Follow up with a thank-you.

Get and Use a Business Card

To you, business cards may seem to be an item that is not necessary immediately or an expense that could wait. Neither excuse is valid. Business cards are necessary for networking. If you want a person to remember you or ever to contact you, a business card is a must. Online services such as Vista.com, overnightprints.com, 123print.com, and printcentric.com produce a limited number of business cards free or for a low fee. In addition, Microsoft and other software programs can produce perfectly acceptable business cards that you can print on your own printer. The only expense is the card stock. Lastly, FedEx shipping stores, Office Depot, Staples, and other office supply stores can print small quantities of cards (250–500) for less than $40.

As a student, you just need what is known as the European-style card, which displays your name, phone number, and perhaps e-mail address centered on the card. You could add your mailing address if you want.

Have an Opening Line: "Breaking the Ice"

An opening is not a standard one-line-fits-all remark. For example, a network opening is not the same type of line you would hear in a bar or at a party in which your interests were other than networking. You cannot use the same icebreaker in every situation, nor do you need a dozen different openings like a set of different clubs for golf. Two or three variations should be sufficient to cover just about all the situations for which you will find opportunities to network.

The most important preparations you can make involve first thinking in advance about what you will say when you meet someone new. This means you need to prepare several different opening lines or icebreakers and try them out on several people. Second, you need to understand the psychology of human contact. By an overwhelming percentage—some experts say 90 percent or more—most human communications are non-verbal. This simply means your initial contact and subsequent follow-up communications with another person will be predominantly conducted through body language, tonality, and neurologic impressions. Further-more, research (from a field called neuroplasticity) indicates that people make micro-judgments about other individuals they see and meet for the first time. These thin slices of rapid cognition constitute a major part of what we call intuition. Much of this takes place in our unconscious brains, but it is a powerful primer for whether you make a "great" or "poor" first impression on someone. The really good news is you have control over this primer. A natural, comfortable, and warm smile with a firm handshake initiates this primer.

It is important to remember that you not only have to develop these ice-breakers but also have to practice, practice, practice. The idea is for your opening line to sound normal and conversational in the given situation and not awkwardly rehearsed or phony. For example, you should have one opening statement for a totally accidental and very brief meeting such as in a hallway, in an elevator, or on an escalator. Another opening statement should be ready for use when you are seated next to a person such as at a meal or in a meeting for which there is a networking opportunity.

A third opening statement could be one you use in a social gathering such as a cocktail reception or trade show exhibit gathering. An ice-breaker is an "opening" and, as such, should focus on the other person, not you. You want to show empathetic skills right off the bat. You are someone who cares about other people, their needs, their time, their problems, and their business. The more you use these opening lines, the easier they will flow out and sound natural. As with any skill you practice, using these opening lines often will make them part of your conversation.

The following lines (preceded with a natural smile and, if appropriate, a handshake) are just some ideas for you to examine and customize for your own style:

- "Hello, my name is _____." You might consider adding "and I'm a student at _____" or "I'm a [senior, junior, business student, etc.]."

- "Are you a member? I'm thinking of joining this [group, organization, class, etc.]."

- "How have you found these [events, programs, activities, etc.]?"

- "What brought you out to this [event, meeting, activity, luncheon, etc.]?"

- "I'm new here. Can you tell me anything about this [group, organization, meeting, activity, etc.]?"

- "I am interested in joining (or becoming a member) of this group, and this is my first [meeting, event, activity, etc.]. How does this compare to others that you have attended?"

- "Have you attended this type of meeting before? What do you think about it?"

- "Have you heard the speaker before? What can you tell me about him or her?"

- "Could you tell me something about this [group, association, society, organization, firm, etc.]?"

- "You appear to know your way around this group. Could you please help me?"

- "I recognize you (or I recognize your company name). Would you mind if I asked you a few questions about how you benefit from this [group, association, society, organization, firm, etc.]?"

If you have not figured it out yet, you should note that effective icebreakers are mostly open-ended questions. These questions require more than a specific one- or two-word answer. An opening line that is a closed-ended question that can be answered with a quick "yes" or "no" leaves you with little room for more discussion, so where do you go from there? The trick is to get the other person talking and to start a conversation. Then you will have broken the ice.

Something else very important happens after you get the other person talking. Research has shown that people generally enjoy talking about themselves. Furthermore, sociologists tell us that when two or more people are engaged in a conversation, the other participants in the conversation think of the person who speaks least as being more intelligent. In addition, listening empathetically helps you build rapport, which is commonly referred to as "chemistry," with the other person.

Your new network contact will be much more responsive if he or she notices that you are actively acknowledging his or her comments. Pay attention to the little things because they can make a major difference in how strongly you are able to continue to prime. For example, most people love to hear their name repeated. You should repeat a person's name upon meeting or being introduced. This repetition of that person's name primes the positive first impression and helps you remember the name. Mentioning the person's name subsequently in the conversation reinforces the prime and adds to the other person's positive feelings. Notice what people say and what they are wearing. Look for clues about their interests and what things appeal to them so these can become points of conversation later.

Develop a 20- to 30-Second Branding Statement (Some People Call This an Elevator Statement)

Be prepared to introduce yourself and answer the question, "What do you bring to the conversation?" Of course, no one is going to say, "So _____, what do you bring to this conversation?" or "What can you do for me?" or "What can you do for my company?" However, if you prepare as though that is what people really are thinking, you will be ready. Think of this as your 20- to 30-second infomercial. It should be clear, concise, enthusiastic (passionate is okay), and memorable. It should give the other person a benefit and encourage him or her to want to know more about you.

This is the most important part of your statement:

> **Your branding/elevator statement should demonstrate that you have the other person's interests, needs, or company in mind.**

Remember, first impressions count, and you have a limited time (under two seconds) to reinforce that first impression. Your branding/elevator statement is the key to opening the potential that can come from each contact.

You have to build a branding/elevator statement just like you would create a mission statement, a goal, or an objective. First, you have to develop a sound strategy.

You need to take an introspective inventory of yourself, including a thorough review and analysis of your background, character, skill set, abilities, knowledge, intellect, interests, worldview, experiences, and all the things that make you unique and differentiated.

Everyone on the planet is unique and differentiated, but we usually don't spend much time thinking about these differences. You may have been brought up to believe you should not talk about yourself. This kind of thinking is self-defeating, and you need to put it aside and spend enough time in self-evaluation to honestly and clearly articulate what makes you special.

You do not need to have a professional psychologist conduct a Myers–Briggs battery of tests to do a self-evaluation. After you generate a list of those things that make you unique and special, you must create your branding statement around those things.

Develop a Sound STRATEGY for Your Branding/Elevator Statement

S = Make your infomercial Short and Succinct.

T = Think of it in advance.

R = Remember the Results you wish to achieve.

A = Be Articulate in your message.

T = Time is of the essence; 30 seconds is the maximum length.

E = Speak with Enthusiasm and Energy.

G = Set a Goal to attain.

Y =Focus on You (the other person), not me. In fact, the rule of thumb is to refer to the other person by name or the pronouns "you" or "yours" in a ratio of at least five to one over personal pronouns "me," "I," or "mine."

Here are several examples of some Branding/Elevator statements. Keep in mind these statements are customized by the situation and context of the meeting:

1. Good afternoon, Mrs. _____, You are one of the most [*pick one*] [recognizable, knowledgeable, successful] leaders of the business community, so please forgive me for this brief interruption of your thoughts. Someone as successful as yourself could really help me in trying to learn more about _____. Would you be kind enough to spend 20 minutes with me to share some of what made you successful? I would be very grateful. I promise

to limit the time to 20 minutes. Could we meet next week? Early or later in the week? Early in the morning may be better.

2. Hello, Mr._____, You are one of the speakers at this event [*pick one*] [I don't want to miss, I intend to hear, I enjoyed very much, whose message resonated deeply.] There is so much to learn about _____. Would you be kind enough to grant me 20 minutes of your time so I could learn more about _____? I promise not to monopolize your time, but I feel like this is a once in a lifetime opportunity and it shouldn't be wasted. I am anxious to learn more. What does your schedule look like for the next couple of days?

3. Good morning, _____, This is a pleasant surprise having the opportunity to meet one of foremost [*pick one*] [leaders, experts, authorities in/on] _____. I don't know how you feel about sharing your keys to success, but you could help me greatly enhance my learning as a student if you would be willing to grant me 20 minutes to meet with you to ask you about _____. Could we do this?

Do Your Research and Know Something About Your Potential Network Associates

When you have a meeting or an appointment with a networking associate, or if you have reason to believe you will meet a key networking associate, research the person and his or her company or organization. Find out as much information as possible about the event you will be attending. The event, the company, and the individual will likely have Web pages, which will have "press room" pages, "event" home pages, "news centers," or "profiles."

Also, look through "history" pages. Check hard-copy sources such as trade magazines, newspapers, and newsletters related to the individual and his or her industry. Keep in mind that you are searching for any and all ways to differentiate yourself from every other contact your network associate meets. Any piece of information that you have that shows your interest, knowledge, or initiative in this person's field begins to create rapport and could lead to the individual building interest in you.

Have a List of "Get-to-Know-You" Questions Prepared and Practiced So You Sound Natural

"Get-to-know-you" questions are different from your opening state-ment or icebreakers in that they focus on the person with whom you are speaking, not an event you both may be attending or a situation you both may be experiencing.

Here is a story about how a get-to-know-you question works. Several years ago, Andrea was in London to give a workshop. When she entered the auditorium to set up, she found the room full of people all sitting quietly in their seats, staring straight ahead. So she asked them if they were all waiting for her session to begin or if they were still spellbound by the last session.

She got a chuckle. As it turned out, they were waiting for her session, which was not scheduled to begin for another 20 minutes. Hearing this, Andrea responded, "Great, there's a chance to get to know your neigh-bors," and it was as though they had been asked to make a presentation.

No one moved. Finally, one man raised his hand and commented, "We don't do that over here." Andrea smiled and said that people don't do much of that in New York either, yet it's a wonderful way to connect with someone, pass the time, and even learn something new about each other.

Andrea knew that people love to follow instructions, so she asked each person to turn to a neighbor and ask the following questions:

- Why did you come to this conference?
- Where do you work, and what do you do?
- Where do you live?
- What other sessions have you attended?
- What do you do when you are not working?
- What do you love about your work?
- What types of projects do you get involved in, and what have you done recently?

At first nothing happened; then in about 30 seconds, they all started talking at once and kept at it. Andrea found it hard to get them to stop so she could start her session, which she did by asking, "Who just met someone interesting?" And, of course, all hands went up. People wanted to share things they had just learned, and they discovered that they had friends in common, interests in common, and some lived in the same neighborhood.

More importantly to their business lives, they met colleagues who could help with their projects, they learned about parts of the company they had never known about, and they learned how they could become a resource to others.

Develop your own set of personal and business-related get-to-know-you questions.

You can use the ones just mentioned as a guide. Add questions related to family, travel, hobbies, favorite books, movies, and other interests. Add business-related questions appropriate to the situation; then try them out at the next gathering of business people you attend. We guarantee you will meet someone interesting.

Develop a List of Idea-Generator Topics ("Small Talk")

Write down ideas as you think of them. Consider keeping a journal organized by topic. Become conversant about current affairs, best-selling books, movies, business news, the stock market, global affairs, and certainly the latest news in certain key industries of interest to you.

Develop some opening lines around these topics:

- What did you think about the State of the Union speech?
- What business authors do you recommend?
- What business journals do you read?
- What kinds of skills do you think hiring managers are looking for today versus ten years ago?
- How do you think the role of managers has changed as a result of the Internet?

- What has changed the most about the [field, industry, or company] since you began?

- What do you think is different about the generation of workers today than the one before (or the one to come)?

- Would you be willing to share some of your ideas about how to achieve success in this field?

- Have you ever considered mentoring a young person?

People love to be asked "what do you think about_____?" questions. Variations include, "What is your opinion?" or "What is your view?"

Get in Line

At any business or social event, there is usually a line at the bar, refreshment table, buffet table, registration desk, coat check, and so on. When you are standing in line, you have a natural opportunity to start a conversation with the person in front or back of you.

Here is an example of how networking while standing in line worked for Andrea.

It was 11:30 a.m., right before lunch, and there was a line in front of the ladies room at the hotel where Andrea was attending a meeting. Andrea noted the name tag of the woman in front of her and realized they would be in the same meeting. Andrea opened the conversation with, "Have you been to these meetings before? And if so, what do you think of them?" As Andrea and the woman chatted, Andrea discovered the woman was the vice president of a cable company. They exchanged business cards, and Andrea promised to send her information about her seminars. Within seven months, the woman had become a client—all because of a conversation begun while waiting for the restroom.

Take a Deep Breath and Dive into a Group

When you are at any gathering, groups will form. Look for a group that looks friendly, wait for an opening, and say something like, "I don't mean to interrupt, but you seem like a friendly group. I'm new here. Would you mind if I joined you?" Who could say no to that? Often, people will respond by saying something like, "That took courage. I admire that. It's nice to meet you."

Andrea and I both have been in situations such as receptions or business affairs where we were corralled by photographers to be part of a group photo for some magazine or newsletter. After everyone smiles for the picture, this is a great opportunity to turn to the group and admit you are new to the event, ask the others if they are members or if they have been before, and use your 30-second branding statement followed by a get to-know-you question.

Approaching a group or an individual is not easy the first few times. Even if you did all the preparation we have suggested, it can still feel uncomfortable. So, give yourself a pep talk!

Write down a couple of positive and interesting things about yourself, such as the following:

- I am glad to be here.

- I am a great listener.

- I am friendly and a great person and eager to learn and meet new people.

- I am learning much about my field and already know a lot about _____.

Then, in your mind's eye, visualize yourself successfully having the kind of networking conversation that will lead to a long-lasting favorable business relationship.

Look for a Designated Host or Greeter and Introduce Yourself

At many functions, a host or greeter or sponsor is responsible for introducing you to others, especially if you are a new member or a guest visiting for the first time. Ask the host for help in meeting people.

Introduce Yourself to the Speaker

If the event you are attending includes a speaker, take the opportunity to tell this individual how much you are looking forward to his or her talk and mention something specific about the topic or the speaker (remember your research). After the presentation, follow up with a note saying how much you enjoyed the talk and mention some helpful bit of information you took away.

Start a Conversation with Your Meal Partner

At a seated meal, the person to your right or left is a logical person to engage. Use your icebreaker opening statements to start a conversation.

Have an Exit Strategy

Even when you are engrossed in a great conversation with someone, it is perfectly polite to leave something for the next time and close your conversation with a follow-up plan so that you can move on and talk with someone else. The other scenario that calls for an exit strategy is if you are talking with someone and you find yourself mentally counting the minutes to get away if the other person appears to be drifting from the conversation.

Here are some lines to practice:

- "It was great meeting you, and hopefully, we can continue our conversation some other time."

- "Thanks for sharing the information about _____. It sounds exciting. Best of continued success."

- "Please excuse me. I see a friend that I would like to say hello to."

- "I have enjoyed hearing about _____. I am sure we will speak again soon."

- "You have been very interesting to speak with. I'll let you have the opportunity to speak with others who will want to meet you."

Set a Goal for Every Event or Activity You Attend

You may have heard this old saying from business: "To improve something, it first has to be counted and measured." If you want to get better at networking, you first have to set a goal for yourself that you want to improve; then you need to set a measurable standard that can be counted and measured against that standard.

We're not talking about something complicated here, just something as easy as "I want to improve my networking skills, and to do this, I will make four new contacts a week for the next three months." Just to give you an idea how powerful this simple goal and standard is, if you were to achieve just 50 percent of this goal, you would make 25 new networking affiliations.

Follow Up with a Note or a Thank-You Note if Appropriate

You can never go wrong by sending a handwritten note to a new networking contact and especially a thank-you note when that is appropriate. This one act will differentiate you more than almost anything you can do.

Summary

These 14 techniques will help you get through any networking event with confidence. When you start practicing and applying them, you will find yourself actually looking forward to networking events as you continue to expand your network and expand and enrich your life.

In the next chapter, you will learn about the kind of people you will want to include in your network.

3

Creating Connections: The People You Need in Your Network

You may say, "I'm still a college student. I don't know that many people who can help me." This is looking at the glass as being half empty.

Henry Ford said, "You can believe that you can succeed or you can believe you can fail. Either way you'll be right."

Unless you have been living alone on a desert island for your entire life up to this moment, you know a lot more people than you think you do, and it is these people, some of whose names you may have to think a little to remember, who will become the core of your created network while you are in college.

Your school classmates should be able to supply a rich source of networking contacts for you. You may not become comfortable seeking network contacts, but your college classmates are a good place to start and succeed. It is indeed a small world. You may have heard the theory in terms of "six degrees of separation," meaning that just about everyone you meet is within six contacts of knowing everyone else. The key here is that you have more contacts than you are aware of, and if you take the time to make these contacts effective assets, the effort will pay off for you and your contacts.

Networking is not just for networking events or for when you are told "it's time to network." Networking is a way of life, a state of mind. You do it all the time without even realizing it. In this chapter, we help you identify the types of people you should include in your network. You will discover that many of them are already in your life.

"I don't have time to network. I'm already too busy to be with my friends and do the things I want to do!" Does this sound familiar? Would you like to know how these people and activities fit right into your busy college life and can be part of your networking success story?

Types of People for Your Network

An important first step for you is to identify the people with whom you want to build a relationship. The types of people you need in your network include the following:

- Fellow students
- Graduates and former students
- Students at other schools
- Instructors
- School administrators
- School staff
- Individuals you have met at seminars, clinics, workshops, conferences, and other events
- Fellow workers
- Coworkers at your last job(s)
- Relatives
- Friends
- People you meet by chance, such as while waiting in lines

- Neighbors
- Like-minded people
- Your medical practitioner(s) and support team
- Your legal and financial service team
- Retail sales clerks and the merchants you buy from
- Ministers, rabbis, and other religious leaders
- People in your address books: texting, smart phone, and cell phone
- Contacts, as well as contacts from Facebook and other social networking sites
- People on your Christmas card list
- People you met at the last five parties you attended
- People at your gym or spa
- People on your sports teams
- The service, repair, and maintenance people who come to your home
- Your barber or hairdresser
- Every professional with whom you come into contact
- Waitresses and waiters
- Members of your church, temple, synagogue, or membership clubs
- Fellow pet owners
- Fellow gamers

It's a Small World, Especially in School

Sabrina slammed her locker shut. Then she slammed the closed door with the flat of her hand, making as unmusical a clang as possible.

"What's the matter?" Juan asked, closing his locker with a bare click.

"I know I'm supposed to be networking, to get with it and connect, but with who? I don't know that many people. I'm falling behind, and I haven't even started. I don't know anyone!"

"How can you say that?" He grinned, probably at how frustrated her face must look. "Look at all the people you know from your Youth Group at church. For the last two years, you told me you've been volunteering at the nursing home near your house and are always telling me how many of the patients and their families you have gotten to know, besides the staff that you always talk about. You must have created a whole group of friends and connections there. What about the Drama club where you have been in two plays and said you've helped out with a dozen more? Think of all the people you've gotten to know through that adventure. Don't forget the International club and those yearly trips you took overseas. I remember you saying you'd made some great friends from these trips and really bonded. And then just last week you told me how you helped one of your friends you met at a History conference. You were able to introduce him to one of your former professors who was very happy to speak with him!"

"Oh," Sabrina felt herself relax. "I guess I let myself wind up and while uptight forgot how many people's lives I have touched, even a little. Maybe I'd better quit making excuses and get reconnecting. And can I count on some of your friends too?"

"You know you can."

* * *

Go back and take a look at all the threads that weave into your current networking fabric and start reaching out, reconnecting, and having conversations to stay in touch. Your potential is limitless when you start to realize that you have been building connections your whole life.

The truth is, almost everyone with whom you come into contact—fellow students, instructors, school staff, friends, graduates, family members, coworkers—knows someone from whom you can learn something that could benefit your job search, your personal life, or even your hobbies and interests. Be sure also to take advantage of the people with whom you created connections through the Internet. With LinkedIn, Facebook, Pinterest, and the host of other social media outlets, you have a whole other component of creating valuable contacts that can turn into strong connections in your network over time. The goal is to keep adding both like-minded people and those you can learn from and give back to.

Look at Figure 3-1 and see the contacts you could continue to add and expand as you build your network.

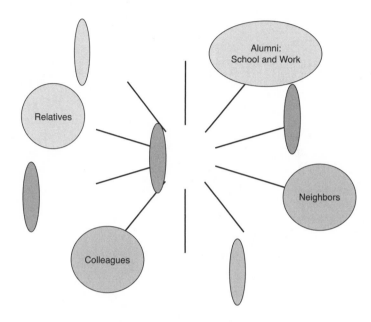

Figure 3-1 Just some of your network possibilities.

Summary

You, like most college students, recent college graduates, and young professionals, have more contacts than you think you have. If you parlay these contacts with your social networking skills, which are easier to learn and sharpen because you have been practicing your learning skills, you can gain a head start in networking.

In the next chapter, you will learn about what makes a great networker.

4

Characteristics of Great Networkers

Do you know someone who can walk into a classroom full of strangers and immediately make friends? Can you recall someone who instantly made you feel at ease when you first met him or her? How about a person who makes you feel as though you are the only person in the world when he or she is speaking to you?

If you know such a person, or people, take a moment to think about what personality traits they possess. Are they confident? Empathetic? Enthusiastic? Energetic? Tenacious? Caring? Appreciative? As you have probably already noted, they are good listeners. Chances are they possess all these qualities—and more. You can possess these characteristics as well, and this chapter focuses on how.

Here you look at each characteristic and explore how it works in effective networking. As with everything you examine here, you can adapt these skills to your own personality, lifestyle, worldview, abilities, and goals as you develop your own networking skills.

Effective networkers are people who connect because they are:

1. Confident

2. Empathetic

3. Appreciative

4. Tenacious

5. Enthusiastic and energetic

6. Caring

7. Rapport builders

Networking and success are connected, and it is not a quirk or coincidence that so many successful people have large, diverse networks. One common characteristic of successful people in many different fields, professions, and walks of life is that they all have built large personal networks.

Networking alone will not make you successful. However, without a network, you are unlikely to achieve a high level of success.

Let's look at the seven characteristics in more detail.

Confidence

Neil is the president of a runner's club that meets for runs on Saturday mornings. He exudes confidence. It shows in how he is able to silence 50 eager runners to make announcements before a run and in how he is able to muster an army of volunteers to raise thousands of dollars for a run to benefit cancer research. His confidence is magnetic. People gravitate to him and eagerly offer their time and expertise. Where did Neil's confidence come from? You can't buy it. If there were a store that sold it, we would all be in line. Confidence comes with experience and grows over time. What kind of experience helps you develop it? Not sitting still. Not doing the same thing repeatedly and expecting different results. To build confidence, you have to step out of your comfort zone and take some risks. It helps to start with small steps and then keep going as your confidence grows.

Almost every college and university has a student activity department responsible for student clubs, organizations, and other activities in which you can become involved. It is in these activities, where your fellow students and friends are, that you can begin the small steps of confidence building.

You can join organizations, go to meetings, take part in committees, do planning work, join the boards, and volunteer to speak, particularly in clubs such as Toastmasters and American Marketing Association chapters. The more active you become, the more confidence you develop in your ability to meet others and speak up.

You will meet John, a student of Michael's, in Chapter 12, "Tying It All Together." He had to step out from his comfort zone to meet and follow up with the people with whom he wanted to connect. He took small steps, made a plan, and before long was choosing between two excellent job offers. John would be the first to tell you he was less than comfortable at first, even reluctant, but he persisted, and the more he tried networking, the better he got. Soon he was confident in his ability to meet and talk with people, and people were eager to meet him. His confidence made him more relaxed and approachable.

Compare this process to any new thing you have mastered, such as learning to play tennis or video games, or speaking in front of a group. You started with small steps and progressed as your competence and confidence grew. Most importantly, you had to step outside your comfort zone, take a risk, do something different. As you continued to practice and got better at the skill, you gained confidence. Did you also notice that people were more interested in what you had to say than before? Expanding your contacts in your field of expertise was suddenly easier.

To develop confidence, practice the skills you want to attain. Over time, the confidence you have developed in your abilities will show. As with

Neil and John, people will be drawn to you because you've become a more confident person.

Empathy

An empathetic person puts himself or herself in another's shoes. Being empathetic does not necessarily mean you share another's point of view; it does, however, mean you are concerned about others and are interested in hearing their point of view.

Some people confuse empathy with sympathy, but they are not the same. The difference between the two is that when you listen to someone with a sympathetic view, you can feel a "temporary" uneasiness for the individual, but it does not reach the level of affecting you personally. In contrast, listening to someone with an empathetic view leaves you with the exact same feeling—good or bad—as the speaker, and you can easily see yourself in the exact same position.

Empathetic people pay attention to the details. They take the time to look and listen to others. They observe and interpret body language. They listen as carefully to what people leave unsaid as to what they say. They have the ability to read between the lines. They can tell when a friend is preoccupied and respect these boundaries. They have the ability to make the other person truly feel he or she is heard and valued.

An example of empathy can be seen in a situation Andrea experienced. She was working at home when she received a call from a business colleague, Susan. Although Susan tried to sound upbeat, Andrea could tell something was not quite right. Susan's voice and speech pattern did not seem normal, and she did not want to discuss anything over the phone, which Andrea respected. However, Andrea suggested coffee the next morning. As it turned out, Susan confided she had lost her job in a sudden dismissal and was in a state of shock and depression.

Andrea listened, observed, and encouraged Susan to begin working on a career plan. Within a week, Andrea received a call from another contact who was looking for a person with skills similar to those of Susan. A few calls, a meeting or two later, and Susan had a new job and career. Andrea's empathetic skills led to the steps necessary to set the ball in motion to make other things happen.

Become Aware of Communication Styles

It is important to understand that for most young adults, their experiences have stopped being something that has happened to them, as when they were adolescents, and instead their experiences have become part of them, a result of their own actions. Thus, young adults define themselves by their experiences. Ignoring or devaluing these experiences has a negative impact on their self-image. Therefore, how different people communicate—how they give and receive information—is an important part of their view of themselves.

Empathetic people are aware of communication styles and will accommodate their style to others when appropriate. Part of adapting a style involves understanding that we all use different styles of communication when giving and receiving information.

Some people are auditory. They learn and communicate best through listening and case discussion. They learn best by hearing information. They prefer a verbal report to a written report. They like to listen to the news rather than read a newspaper. When you are speaking with an auditory-type person, it makes sense to check in with the person using check phrases such as "Are we in harmony?" "Are we connecting?" "Are we in sync?" or "How does this sound to you?"

Some people are visual. They learn through watching, observing, and reading. They need to see pictures or "see it in writing." These are the folks who take lots of notes in lectures and treasure the handouts. These people love visuals, PowerPoint slides and other types of presentations, and flipcharts. When visual-type individuals communicate, they often draw what they are talking about on a pad or whiteboard. To connect with them, you might use phrases such as "How does this look to you?" or "Picture this."

The third major learning approach is kinesthetic—learning through doing, practicing, or touching. These people need to act things out or have things demonstrated to them. They are likely to talk with lots of hand and arm motion, lots of gestures and animation. They learn best actually doing or taking part. Checking phrases for these people might include "Are you comfortable with this?" or "How does this feel to you?"

Adjust to the Personality Styles of Others

In addition to being aware of communication styles, empathy requires adjusting yourself to other people's orientation. Some people are more oriented or sensitive to the concerns and feelings of others, other people are more "bottom line" or results oriented, and still others are interested and concerned with details and the way things work. Obviously, this description is a simplification of the complex concept of personality styles and behavior types. Study this concept if you are interested; however, to be empathetic, you really just need to listen carefully and respect the other person's orientation.

Andrea once worked on presenting a business proposal to three different decision makers within a single organization. She knew from previous conversations that she was dealing with three different personality styles and that to be successful she would need to show empathy and be oriented toward three completely different individuals.

The human resources director was harmonious and amiable in her approach. She had mentioned to Andrea that she wanted to "make sure to get everyone involved." Caring and concern were important, as was emphasizing the human element. In this case, Andrea had to focus her presentation on the personal benefits for the employees.

The chief financial officer, on the other hand, was primarily interested in the return on investment he would get from Andrea's program. He also wanted lots of details. In this presentation, the more detailed the data, the better the client liked it.

Lastly, the chief executive officer had only five minutes to give. All he wanted to know was "What are my people going to learn?" and "How much is this going to cost?" In this presentation, Andrea just answered those two questions, providing a short, succinct "bottom line" summary.

In this case, there were three very different people, all wanting basically the same information but in vastly different ways. For Andrea to succeed, she had to deliver the information in the way each person needed it.

An empathetic person is an excellent listener who understands and adapts to the needs of others. Being empathetic does not mean you have to change your personality; nor does it mean being solicitous, weak, or manipulative. It is a positive, sincere, and proactive approach to under-standing another's feelings, interests, and needs.

The definition of empathy is "the action of understanding [and] being aware of the feelings, thoughts, and experience of another...without having the feelings, thoughts, and experience fully communicated in an objectively explicit manner." Therefore, to become empathetic, you need to be aware of communication styles and personality types.

Appreciation

The quality that makes people, and will make you, a more charismatic networker is the natural instinct to give sincere appreciation. We believe you can never tell someone "thank you" too many times when it is done sincerely.

There are many ways to say thank you. The one that says it the most effectively, according to most surveys on the topic, is the handwritten thank-you note sent via the U.S. Postal Service. Now there is digital technology that allows you to use a font that appears handwritten even though a note is typed; thus, you gain the efficiency of digital com-munications and the personalization of the U.S. Postal Service. Thank-you notes can be sent by e-mail, which is quick, easy, and immediate. However, the recipient can delete e-mail messages even before they are opened, so there is a chance your thank-you note might not be recog-nized. A handwritten note is unlikely to be discarded before it is read.

There is also the face-to-face thank you, delivered sincerely with special emphasis on the communication style of the person you are appreciat-ing. You can also show your appreciation by sending a small gift. We are big believers in giving gifts, and Andrea will share some of her tech-niques when you get to Chapter 7, "Keeping Your Network Alive and Growing."

Saying thank you may seem to be rather simple etiquette—a no-brainer—yet it is amazing how few people remember to take the action and how positive an impact the action has when taken. It can do wonders for your professional and personal growth as a networker.

Andrea once received a voice-mail message that confirmed the value of saying thank you. The message was from a CEO of a company for whom she had done some programs. His message was, "I want to thank you and compliment you on the work you've been doing for us. I would also like to share some of the flattering remarks that several people have for you...." Although the CEO took just 30 seconds in his busy day to make the phone call, it had such an impact on Andrea that she left the message on her answering machine for several weeks.

We all strive to be remembered positively by others. Showing sincere appreciation always makes a lasting impression. People want to do business with people (and hire people) they enjoy being with and will seek them out. In addition, an affirming communication has a way of leading to other opportunities.

Here is how a personal expression of gratitude led Andrea to a referral and a new client. Andrea had thanked one of her suppliers for helping her meet a near-impossible deadline. The supplier said he wanted to do something in return. He told her about another one of his clients he thought might need Andrea's services, and he gave her the referral. She followed up and got the new business—all from a simple thank you.

Tenacity

At least 20 percent of Andrea's business has come from people who turned her down the first time. When she realized this, it was a lesson to her that being tenacious could pay off for networking and for business.

Andrea recalls how one current customer was particularly tough to win over. She called on this client for three years and went nowhere. No one even returned her calls. The direct approach clearly was not working, so she decided to network her way to the client. Andrea thought about the client and what organizations, events, activities, and clubs this client might belong to or attend. There is an old saying that applies to this strategy: "If you want blueberries, go to where the blueberries grow." So Andrea went to where the blueberries grew. She belonged to several business networking groups and thought it might be possible the client would attend one of these groups.

At least, Andrea reasoned, if the client didn't attend, someone from her firm might attend. The break came when Andrea was giving a presentation at a meeting of one of the groups. After the presentation, a woman from the target client's firm approached and suggested Andrea meet with someone in her firm who could use Andrea's services. The woman offered to set up the meeting. Guess who that someone turned out to be? None other than Mrs. "Never Returns My Calls."

The story does not have a happy ending just yet. Andrea and the prospective client did meet, and at first, Andrea could tell the woman was doing it out of courtesy for her coworker and really did not want to meet with her. However, things got better as the meeting progressed, and the meeting ultimately went from the 20 minutes the woman originally had allotted to an hour and a half. At the end of the meeting, she told Andrea she liked the proposal, but frankly it took five years for outside consultants to land work in the firm. She did tell Andrea to call quarterly just to stay in touch. At first, Andrea was discouraged, but then she thought, at least she got in the door and now she had five years to go, so she had better hang in there. Andrea sent a handwritten thank-you note, and a month later when the woman was promoted, Andrea sent a note of congratulations.

When the first quarter was up, Andrea called and left this message: "I know I still have four and three-quarters years left. I am just touching base." Andrea continued to keep in touch for two quarters, and then to her surprise, the woman called. Andrea was awarded not one but two projects with the firm. In the time since, Andrea has done more than 30 projects for this firm, which is one of her largest clients. Tenacity paid off. Rather than getting discouraged about the five-year timetable, Andrea just put it on her schedule to call every quarter and stayed in touch.

Tenacity and patience sometimes make good partners. When Michael was nearing the end of his active duty in the U.S. Marine Corp, he took advantage of a training program and became a licensed 35-mm motion picture projector operator. He worked his last few months in the Marines running a base movie theater projector operation in the evenings. He knew he was going to college upon his discharge, and the new skill offered a possible job while going to school. According to union scale, motion picture projector operators were very well paid. Michael was discharged from the Marines and returned to St. Louis to begin community college. As it turned out, the union opportunities in the movie theaters were very lucrative but only if your family was in the business already. Michael took his skill to a private professional audio-visual firm and worked for that firm while attending community college. Michael kept in contact with the president of that firm even when he moved to New Jersey to continue work on his B.A. degree.

Upon graduation from college, Michael returned to St. Louis. He contacted the president of the audio-visual firm who was happy to give Michael whatever temp work he could, but it was clear Michael was way overqualified for anything full time. A week after returning, Michael got a call from the regional sales manager of the Dun & Bradstreet (D&B) office, who told him he was the next-door neighbor of the president of the audio-visual firm. The two men had been talking over their backyard fence the night before, and the D&B manager had mentioned how much he needed someone and how he did not want to put out a "general casting call." The president of the audio-visual firm had given him Michael's resume, and he made the call. Michael went in for the interview and was hired that day. Michael spent 20 years with D&B. Tenacity and patience were partners in the outcome.

One additional story will strengthen the point about keeping up your networking even within your company. Michael was very disciplined about extending his networking inside D&B because the same rules and opportunities apply inside a firm as they do to your general network. After ten years, Michael left D&B for another career opportunity with the Direct Marketing Association (DMA). Several years later, he returned to D&B through a contact with an individual he had kept in his network.

After 5 years, he took a buyout with several thousand other employees but returned a month later to a different D&B division, again as a result of a networking contact. All in all, he spent 20 years with D&B. When he left D&B for the last time, he moved to a senior position, by way of a networking contact, back to DMA.

Tenacity, patience, and keeping his options open: Each move to each organization resulted in a promotion, more compensation, and a wider, more fulfilling network.

There is a fine line between being tenacious and being a pest. Be careful not to cross the line. Much of knowing where that line ishas to do with getting permission to keep in touch. In the "five-year case," Andrea knew her initial meeting had gone well, and, because the woman had invited her to keep in touch, it was appropriate to follow up with the phone calls and notes. Being tenacious is a positive way of taking advantage of opportunities, as well as looking at the setbacks that come along as opportunities in disguise and keeping at it.

It may seem counterintuitive, but we know from research and experience that people who are asked for help, if they decide to help, will take a deep personal interest in the person who has asked for the help. It is as though they have an emotional and psychological investment in the person and want to protect their investment and ensure that it pays off. Being tenacious (and not pushy) is giving people something in which they can invest and engage.

Enthusiasm and Energy

Enthusiasm and energy are contagious. When you are enthusiastic, you bring out the enthusiasm in others. If you are full of energy, the energy in the space around you rises.

If you need proof, watch what happens at a gathering when folks are waiting for a speaker to take the floor. If the speaker arrives with energy, watch how the expressions on the audience members' faces change and the room becomes "charged." The experiment with one person controlling the mood of a group has been conducted so often that the results have become rather predictable. In control groups, one person is preselected to be either a mood depressor or a mood elevator. All it takes is one person with the right dynamics, and that one person can change the mood of an entire group either in a positive or negative direction. Jury selection experts have known about this dynamic for years and know that one person can project a certain mood or feeling, and the first "straw" vote is an excellent indicator of the final jury vote.

Viewed in a positive way, you can alter the impression people have of your intelligence just by your level of enthusiasm. We know that high levels of enthusiasm are often mistaken for high levels of intelligence.

By being highly enthusiastic, you not only raise the level of enthusiasm of others around you, but also increase the possibility that others may believe you are more intelligent than you are. There is nothing wrong in that. Enthusiasm also makes people more receptive to your message.

Realize, though, that enthusiasm and energy come in many forms. You do not have to be loud and excited to be energetic or enthusiastic. Enthusiasm can be a quiet passion that shines and makes people want to be a part of it.

Caring

When you truly care about others and you don't expect a payback for your efforts, you indeed get the ultimate reward. You make others feel good about themselves and about you. Often the very act of caring produces unexpected, positive networking results.

Recently, Andrea received one of those "voices from your past" phone calls. It was from Gloria, who had been the receptionist at a company Andrea had called on to sell advertising space years ago. It had been 14 years since Andrea had last seen her. Gloria was vice president of marketing for another company. She had recently read an article Andrea had written and decided to call about doing a project for her new company. Andrea was flattered by the call and her invitation to do the project. When Andrea asked what made her call, Gloria said that Andrea had always made her feel important when visiting the firm, and even told the then-president of the firm that she had a great voice and a smile that truly came across on the phone. Gloria told Andrea she always wanted to return the kindness. Effective networkers are always networking not because they "need" to; rather, they network to create lifelong connections with people. They embrace networking as a way of life. They network without the thought of getting an immediate or specific payback.

Effective networkers know they are making positive connections in which all parties ultimately benefit. How very different this is from the image many people hold of networkers, whom we refer to as "pathological networkers"—individuals who engage in "negative networking." These individuals never think of picking up the telephone, writing a personal note, sending an e-mail, or extending a helping hand until they need something. They are not networking.

Rapport Building

Have you ever been in a situation in which you have just met someone face-to-face and felt an instant bond, or been introduced to someone in a group and felt you somehow "connected" with that person more so than others in the group? That spontaneous or instant appeal is called rapport. It is identified by both verbal and nonverbal body language.

The verbal communications include forms of agreements and elaborations and requests for more information. Showing rapport with language includes such phrases as the following:

- "I see what you mean."
- "I understand."
- "I get the picture."
- "I hear what you're saying."
- "That sounds right to me."
- "That rings true to me."
- "That clicks with me."
- "That resonates with me."
- "I like your idea."
- "It makes sense to me."

Or the person wanting to show rapport may probe with questions such as the following:

- "Could you elaborate on that point?"
- "Can you clarify that?"
- "I would like to know more about that. Could you be more specific?"
- "Could you break that down into smaller pieces for me?"
- "Could you walk me through that again?"

Nonverbal body language includes more intense eye contact, head and upper body movement toward you, open hand gestures, smiling, and light hand touching of the arm or shoulders.

Rapport is critical because it leads to influence and a natural bridge to networking and the other six behavior patterns of people who are effective networkers.

Selecting and Working with Mentors

One of the most valuable experiences you can receive is a mutually beneficial affiliation with an experienced network of qualified, professional, motivated mentors. The classic old-school model of the mentor–protégé relationship was based on a senior executive selecting a junior colleague to take under his or her wing.

Under this networking model, the protégé is guided in job choices, career direction, promotion options, business etiquette and culture, even social and lifestyle issues. The traditional mentor would remain close to the protégé throughout the younger person's career. Often the two careers would be linked, and if not the actual careers, the individuals would be.

Today, the model has changed dramatically. Mentors and protégés still exist, but the environment of the classic model has all but disappeared. The executives of today's flatter, faster-paced organizations do not have the time or resources to support protégés. In addition to a more hurried business life, many business executives have to pay renewed attention to their own careers. Furthermore, today's younger workers do not need advice on achieving long-term success within specific organizations or industries. The focus is on their personal development in a changing working environment and an evolving economic climate.

Young workers know that one person cannot help with all the issues, questions, and networking needed today. Therefore, the more practical approach for the contemporary protégé is a stable of mentors. Instead of being selected by a senior executive, today's protégé needs to take control of the process and seek out a team of mentors in different fields, specialties, knowledge areas, disciplines, professions, and industries. With this approach, the young worker gains a heterogeneous and diverse set of opinions, views, and recommendations that meet the situational circumstances of today's young workers, which can and do change rapidly.

To begin building a stable of mentors, recognize that they do not have to be a separate group from your regular network—just individuals you have identified and targeted for extra special attention. Certain special skills are called on to develop this mentor group, such as being tenacious, enthusiastic, and effective at building rapport.

The key in adapting to the current model is the emphasis on the protégé being proactive. All the rules and techniques we mention apply to the mentor selection, but we want to emphasize how important it is to be proactive. You are in a competitive environment. No one is going to "discover" you. No one will suddenly become aware of your great potential, approach you, and volunteer to mentor you. You must initiate the contact and reach out to those whose help you want.

You are competing not only with your peers but also with the time and resources of the targeted mentor. You cannot be coy or shy about identifying and approaching someone who will be willing to support your career development and give you advice, feedback, information, insight, and other forms of help. Pay close attention to how a contact relates and builds rapport with you, as well as you with the contact.

If you pick up on signs that the person is willing to be helpful, test the waters with requests for information and advice to see how he or she responds. Without being overbearing, you need to be tenacious about starting and building a protégé–mentor relationship. You may need to take a more assertive lead in setting up planned meetings, such as coordinating specific days and times and places for coffee or meals. Don't be afraid to take a leadership position and offer to make arrangements for the meeting from which you will be gaining great benefit.

Of course, in a mentor–protégé relationship, the frequency of contact is greater than in the normal networking relationship. However, do not confuse simple instant messaging (IM) or text messages, sent on a frequent basis with no real purpose other than real-time communications for the sake of real-time communications, with mentor–protégé contacts.

When you do meet your mentor in person or online, make sure you have researched and responded to his or her previous requests. Always follow up and remind your mentor that you have found what he or she had requested. Of course, it is better to have found more and to have exceeded your mentor's expectations.

Whenever possible, try to share personal information with your mentor. The one thing that has not changed in the mentor–protégé relationship is that once a person has accepted the mentor's role, he or she feels personally responsible for the protégé's success. The mentor appreciates information and details that provide a connection to his or her role. You don't have to share intimate personal details or secrets, but do share information that opens a bridge and helps create a stronger bond.

Lastly, always be personable and enthusiastic. Mentors, like almost everyone else, prefer to work with people who exude a positive attitude.

Summary

When you have developed and practiced the traits of an effective networker, and you suddenly do find yourself in a job hunt situation or need a business contact or need business leads or need other business assistance, you will have no problem contacting people who will be more than glad to lend you a helping hand. They will listen and offer sound advice, opportunities, and real referrals. Nonstop networking does work. Make nonstop networking your way of life.

In the next chapter, you will learn tips for helping people who may be shy or self-conscious with becoming successful networkers.

When Networking Doesn't Come Easy: Networking for Introverts

The more you network, the more you will come into contact with different types of personalities and their varying styles of networking. Two very different types of people can approach a room full of people from completely different perspectives and achieve the same results.

One can work the room in a gregarious manner, meeting many different people and engaging in multiple conversations, whereas another can be quieter, engaging in fewer, more engrossing conversations. However, when they walk out of the meeting, they both have found new contacts, made new friends, made contacts, and secured referrals and leads.

The differences in their approach to networking are a result of their personality traits. The first person, the gregarious one, is more of an extrovert; extroverts get their energy from being around and interacting with people. The second person is more of an introvert; introverts gather their energy internally.

The Introvert's Networking Advantage

Many introverts, such as the one just described, are good networkers. They know how to use their introverted nature to their advantage. They are often good listeners. They notice details and remember important facts, and because introverts often let others do more talking, the other person walks away thinking the introvert was a brilliant conversationalist. There is also research data that shows when one person has done the majority of the listening, people who have observed the conversation as well as the speaker believe the listener is the more intelligent of the two.

Introverts are also more thoughtful and frequently the first to give compliments, to remember special events, and, of course, to remember to say thank you. Remember the preceding chapter and the critical importance of the seven characteristics of great networkers? Three of the characteristics are common in introverts—empathy, appreciation, and caring. So, if you are, or suspect you are, an introvert, the first step is to understand and appreciate your best qualities and learn how to use them to your advantage in networking.

Thoughtful Listening

Listening carefully to others is a skill most extroverts need to work on. It comes easier to introverts, who naturally absorb and use what they hear. Introverts generally spend more time listening and less time talking.

Andrea knows a really great communicator, Alice. Every time they meet, Alice mentions something she remembers about Andrea from a prior conversation. Not long ago, Andrea and Alice were meeting about a project when Alice began a conversation by asking about Andrea's sister

Meredith and her horse Noddy. Not only did Alice remember Andrea's sister's name but also that she had a horse and the horse's name. Alice is an example of an excellent listener. She remembers details and puts the skill to work effectively. She is someone who epitomizes what we call a good networker. She listens, she takes in all sorts of information, and when the time is right, she puts different people and projects together where she thinks there is a good fit. If she were asked, Alice would say she is a total introvert and not a good networker. Andrea thinks differently.

Here are some other common but bad listening habits to avoid:

- Focusing on the other speaker rather than what he or she is actually saying

- Ignoring or shutting out what you don't understand or don't like

- Letting your emotions bias or filter what the other person is saying

- Daydreaming or letting external environmental factors distract you

- Interrupting before the speaker is finished

Good listeners engage in active emphatic listening. Normal American conversational speech is about 25 words per minute. Normal comprehension, on the other hand, can occur at 400 to 500 words per minute. In other words, you are capable of listening at a rate many times faster than the other person is capable of speaking. This is nothing to celebrate. It's the reason for the most common bad listening habit—daydreaming. When you listen to someone speaking at a speed that's only about a portion of your listening capability, your mind tends to fill its leftover capacity with other things. These other things can then crowd out the conversation, and you lose some of what's being said.

The cure for this inevitable tendency of the mind to wander during conversation is a discipline called active listening. Active listening is a way of giving your mind jobs to do that are concerned with the conversation. These jobs keep it focused.

Following are three techniques that you may want to consider as skill builders for better listening.

First Technique: Playing Back

One of the most powerful listening strategies is the technique of playing back. Listen to what the other person says and play it back. This technique is particularly useful in a networking situation for introverts because it helps you check your interpretation of what the other person has said, and it actually makes him or her feel good. Beyond that, however, it is powerful because it forces you to process what the other person says. You can't simply repeat back the other person's own words, although you sometimes may want to do that. To keep the conversation moving, you need to deal with the meaning of what the other person says. Playing back has the additional benefit of opening up the other person. Everyone has a desire to be understood, and playing back what the other person has said almost invariably encourages the person to provide additional information.

Second Listening Technique: Summarizing

Summarizing is like playing back, except that it happens less frequently and it involves more than one thought. As you process what the other person is saying, fit it together so you can summarize a list of points the person has made. Like playing back, this technique has benefits at two different levels:

1. It lets you check your understanding.

2. It forces you to attend to what the other person is saying so you can create the summary later.

At various points in the conversation, use a lead-in phrase and then list the points the other person has made: "If I have heard you correctly, you believe..."

Summarizing shows the other person that you are listening, and that's an important part of building the relationship.

Third Listening Technique: Reflecting Emotion

Reflecting is a form of playing back, but it applies to emotions rather than facts.

Whenever you hear a sign of emotion in the other person's conversation, you may want to acknowledge it. This shows the other person that you are attending to him or her as a person, and it builds your relationship.

One of the best lead-in phrases for reflecting emotion is "It sounds like...." For example, you may say, "It sounds like you're angry about the way that turned out."

But there are others you can use for variety, such as the following:

- "I get the sense you're...."
- "I hear _____ in your voice."

Passion

Although many introverts don't relish the idea of walking up to a stranger and starting a conversation, when you get them on a topic they are passionate about, their shyness magically disappears.

When you can focus on an aspect of business, industry, or a product or service you are especially passionate about, you will naturally speak with enthusiasm and conviction. Andrea recalls a conversation with an account executive who told her he became so nervous before meeting with a prospective client that he felt nauseous. Yet as soon as he started talking about his product, the benefits of which he truly believed in, he felt comfortable and at ease. Introverts need a focus and a genuine reason to make a contact.

Eleven Networking Techniques for the Quiet Networker

Under certain circumstances, most of us do feel shy, reticent, or introverted, regardless of what label you put on it. Half of us feel shy all the time, and the other half, part of the time.

We've all felt stuck in the doorway thinking, "Should I walk into that crowded room or go back to my hotel room (or dorm room or home)?" Yet we know that one key component of successful networking is visibility. You can't get visibility in a hotel room or dorm room or bedroom, unless you are networking over the Internet (more on that later in this chapter).

Networking is all about making connections, building relationships, and developing advocates—people who know you and know what you do and what you are capable of doing so that they can become your marketers.

The following sections provide 11 tips on how to successfully network even when you are feeling introverted.

Have an Objective

Be truthful with yourself. Too much self-improvement advice begins with "goal setting" only, and no progress is ever achieved because goals are long term, are ethereal in nature, and have no quantitative measurements. Instead, set objectives that are short term, goal oriented, measurable, and meaningful. Set goals for opportunities you have to expand or to nurture your network; then set achievable measurable objectives that can be counted:

- When attending a networking event, set an objective to meet and follow up with at least two people. By "follow up," we mean within a week you have sent a follow-up e-mail or made a follow-up telephone call.

- At a school or university, set an objective to sit next to someone new. Think of three questions you can ask to learn about each person and his or her background and interests.

- Once a week, go through your contact list or social networking resource, and set an objective to select four to six individuals to e-mail or call. The contacts should be individuals you have not heard from recently. Use the opportunity to "check in" to say hello and ask how they are doing and what they are doing.

- Set an objective to once a month have breakfast or lunch with a friend, colleague, or associate, particularly someone you have not seen for a while.

Take Baby Steps

The concept of networking, or building your network, can seem daunting when you look at it as a "big picture." However, when you break down a project or objective into smaller pieces, you can approach it bit by bit. It is like the adage, "How do you eat an elephant? One bite at a time." Or the advice of an ancient Chinese proverb, "The journey of a thousand miles begins with but a step." If eating an elephant or taking a journey of a thousand miles seems like a daunting task (even the first bite or the first step), you can understand why people who don't network don't like elephant meat or don't travel much.

THE POWER OF A SMILE

When you're standing in the doorway, a networking event can seem scary. So take it step by step. Start by smiling. When you enter a room, whether you are aware of it or not, you are being observed and judged. People make what scientists call microevaluations, or what you might call "snap judgments." Humans have done it for thousands of years, and it is part of our evolutionary development; therefore, please, no moral judgments, just acceptance of the practice. In less than a second, people form what amounts to a full profile of you. They create a lasting impression of your intelligence, worldview, likability, and a wide range of characteristics. Don't worry; you do the same thing. We all do it.

It is up to you to make this initial image as strong as possible, and you can do this with an opening smile—the strongest, most positive non-verbal message known to human beings. If you don't smile, the initial impression will almost always be neutral to negative, and you've started with an unnecessary hill to climb. So, make it as easy on yourself as possible—SMILE!

Establish eye contact with people in the room. You have heard the old saying, "The eyes are the windows to the soul." Well, the eyes are also the door to a conversation. You can tell if someone is receptive to a conversation just by glancing into his or her eyes. We won't try to explain the analytical and clinical reasons behind this phenomenon here, but try looking into the other person's eyes, and you will soon find it works. You must experience it, and you will recognize the person's level of receptiveness when you see it.

Use Lots of Open-Ended Questions

When you meet someone, whether you just go up and introduce yourself or whether someone introduces himself or herself or whether a third party makes the introduction, repeat the name of the person you have just met. Repeating helps you remember the name. Next, to help get the conversation going, you can ask an open-ended question. As discussed in Chapter 2, "Positioning Yourself and Your Brand, 'You,'" an open-ended question is one for which the response cannot likely be a short one- or two-word answer (definitely not a "yes" or "no" question).

Socrates was a master at this kind of question. He would ask questions of people because he truly was interested in assisting them. Open-ended questions help you to surrender control of the moment. Open-ended questions don't just give the other person a choice of responses; instead, they really allow the person to tell you what is going on in his or her mind.

The characteristics of open-ended questions are that they:

- Surrender control of the conversation (or confirm the other person's control)

- Tend to lead to longer responses, which provide you more information about the other person's interests and feelings

- Often include answers involving emotions that you can feed back

Begin with a Compliment

Complimenting someone is a wonderful way to start a conversation. Everyone loves to be complimented on something. Find something sincere to compliment people on any time you have an opening to start a conversation.

Use a Script

If calling back to follow up on a new contact makes you a bit nervous, develop a short yet detailed script to use. Write the key points and rehearse the script until it comes across naturally. Besides your script, have notes to refer to about the person you are calling. After you do this a few times, it may become second nature to you and you can get by with just your notes. Using a script is a good way to develop confidence.

It is also a good idea to always keep a mirror in front of your phone so that you can make sure you are smiling while you are talking. Remember the benefit of the smile? The other person knows whether or not you are smiling.

Work on Your Eye Contact

Recognize that not making eye contact is a mistake and has a disastrous effect. Not only does it give the impression that you are not listening or paying attention, but the person with whom you are speaking may consider you rude. Even worse, avoiding eye contact can be interpreted as a sign that you have something to hide.

Andrea worked with a skilled executive named Ed who was a thoughtful and caring person. However, his colleagues and employees were concerned that he was not listening to them or giving them his full attention because when they spoke to him, he looked off to the side. Andrea confronted Ed with this information, and Ed told her he was shy and felt uncomfortable looking people directly in the eye. This feeling is common for shy or introverted people, but the results of not looking people in the eye are more devastating for establishing relationships.

Because establishing direct eye contact was so awkward for Ed, Andrea suggested a technique called the "third eye approach," which involves looking at a spot just above and between the other person's eyes. Over time, Ed became more and more comfortable at looking people directly in the eye. The results were amazing. People warmed up to him, his confidence grew, and his network expanded.

Attend Events and More Events

You can learn only by doing. Just reading this book alone will not make you a better networker. You have to get out and attend events where you can meet people. Naturally, you may be inclined to start at your own school or university and attend social functions. This is okay for a start and okay to continue as a regular practice, but you need to spread your wings and attend many other functions.

Every community and many regional organizations hold regular functions for networking. Sources include the local Chamber of Commerce, the Better Business Bureau, community development groups, business development and economic development organizations, sales and marketing clubs, speaker clubs, and the list goes on and on. The local papers list these events, as do the Web sites of the various organizations. These groups sponsor breakfast, lunch, and dinner meetings as well as cocktail receptions and other social events in which people gather for the express purpose of networking.

You have to find these events and attend. Students who attend and network these events will have a distinct advantage over their peers and classmates who do not. The reason is simple. The business decision makers, the employers, and the deal makers attend these events, and the students who meet and network with these influencers will be remembered when opportunities arise. Students who do not network simply will not be in the mix and will have to get in line with the hundreds of other sheep.

Set Up One-on-One Meetings

Next time you go to a networking event (or to any event), make it a networking opportunity. Give yourself an objective to connect with just one person and set up a follow-up, one-on-one meeting. Make this meeting at a comfortable place and at a time when you both can relax and get to know one another.

Coffee shops are good venues; no one will rush you, and many have comfortable seating arrangements conducive to conversations. It is much easier to get to know someone in this atmosphere than at events and other get-togethers.

Do Your Networking at Your Highest Energy Level Time of Day

We all have a time of day when we feel more energized, when our circadian rhythms are peaking. If possible, set up meetings, make phone calls, attend events, even do your follow-up e-mails and thank-you notes during these high-energy times. This may not be possible if you have to attend an evening meeting and you are a morning person, but you can still deal with it. Pace yourself during the day (or even take a quick "power nap") to conserve your energy for later when you need it. The important thing is to know your own cycles and prepare ahead of time.

Set a Time Limit

One "quiet networker" Andrea knows gave this advice on dealing with networking events: Set a time limit and say to yourself, "I'll go to the meeting for one hour, and then I will go back and relax." She feels she can successfully gather her energy for an hour, whereas a full evening would be overwhelming. By using this strategy (small baby steps), she gets herself to the meetings knowing it is "only for an hour." Use this tactic in making calls. Decide how much time you will give to the task and stick to it. Don't be unrealistic; start small and remember to take baby steps. When you achieve your objective, you will be energized to continue on or to go longer the next time.

Recharge and Reward Yourself

Plan a schedule so you have time to recharge and reward yourself. This tip is particularly important for college students who may be working full or part time and going to school. You are not invincible and need to recharge your batteries from time to time.

So, do something nice for yourself. Reward yourself for accomplishing each objective you set and for achieving each "baby step" along the way. You deserve a reward, even if it is as small as reaching around and patting yourself on the back.

Networking on the Internet

Online social networking is an efficient way to establish and maintain relationships with others in your field. With the help of the Internet, you will find it easy to locate and meet people on social networking sites who can help you with contacts that can then be helpful in job searches, sales leads, and other business contacts.

Online social networking communities vary by their purpose and demographics, but the digital technologies of LinkedIn, Facebook, MySpace, Twitter, hi5, Friendster, Flickr, Orkut, Bebo, Ning, Doostang, and

Tagged, along with other types of Web 2.0 technologies such as wiki sites, RSS, and blogs, can create collaboration capabilities spanning time and distance barriers. Online technologies are a support tool for networking. Some reports have cited that as many as 60 percent of Americans are online applying digital technology for social networking. While no one can deny the great efficiency of digital technologies for social contacts, the major drawback is the lack of face-to-face contact. There is no way any number of digital contacts can replace the high value of a face-to-face approach.

Remember reciprocity—the creation and development of human trust—begins with face-to-face contact. Not only must the face-to-face contact occur, but the all-important nonverbal communication of body language initiates unconscious mental activity that helps identify positive or negative signals that sometimes only our unconscious mind can detect. Without face-to-face connections, people can build false personas, lie, or otherwise deceive online without your really knowing.

Too many people use the social networking sites in a ubiquitous, incessant, compulsive drive to make dozens to hundreds of microdigital touches that are passed off as social networking. Real networking begins and has a foundation in face-to-face encounters. Digital social networking should be viewed as a support and supplement to face-to-face networking. The daily (and sometimes hourly or more frequent) check-in or shout-out contacts are a form of social contact different from networking and should be viewed and treated differently.

There is no question that some people gain some traditional networking benefits from the microcontact approach, but the personal ties are weak, and if not reinforced by face-to-face encounters, no long-term trust or reciprocity will be established.

According to a Forrester Research study, nearly 60 percent of teenagers (12- to 17-year-olds) and 80 percent of young adults (18- to 21-year-olds) use social networking sites. This contrasts dramatically with only 31 percent of adults (older than 21 years of age) who use social networking sites. Furthermore, only 20 percent of the adults who do use the social networking sites use them for social networking. The frequency of use further shows the demarcation of use by age. Teenagers (60 percent) and young adults (67 percent) use social networking sites with such frequency that their usage creates real-time communications channels once reserved for the telephone and then e-mail.[1] The sheer ubiquity of the use pattern has created a real-time communications channel and altered the social value of the channel for really effective networking.

First, think of your use pattern. Networking contacts do not need to be made daily or two to four times a week like the contact pattern of many ultra-active people on the social networking sites. If ultra-active social media people envision their current contact patterns on social networking sites as effective networking, they could be building a straw man.

Even with dozens or hundreds of "peer" contacts, this kind of group is little more than a somewhat socially compatible group. Even if you imagine it to be a networking group, the makeup of the group is more than likely a homogeneous peer group, and such groups are susceptible to groupthink and groupspeak—too many similar ideas, too many similar beliefs, too many similar views, too much consistency, and not enough diversity of opinions, which is important for your intellectual growth.

The second impact of the ubiquitous use of social networking sites by your generation is the altered social value of the channel for really effective networking. The autonomy of the Internet seems to appeal particularly to your generation because you do not have to worry about the commitment that you sense exists in e-mails and phone calls. This concern, expressed by many of you, will have to be managed, particularly as you need to communicate with other generations in mentoring, job search endeavors, and other networking activities.

If your goal, as it should be, is to break into the business or professional worlds or a larger, more diverse social universe, you need a network populated by the people who are influential, powerful, and/or leaders in these areas—not just fellow students.

The Forrester research data show that these people are not likely to populate the same social networking sites as your peers and that even those who do are in such small numbers that they can't do you much good. It is the larger world you are trying to join and become a part of, not the other way around.

So, for better or worse, you must adapt and expand your reach so that your network reaches the world(s) you want to move into. The autonomy of the Internet also makes it easier for introverts to make new connections, especially with the capabilities of online sites to create "special interest" communities. No one can see how nervous you are or notice you standing off in the corner. You can contact almost anyone you want to meet through e-mail, and this type of communication is easier and faster than playing phone tag. Furthermore, you do not have to create a script or practice before calling. Just be sure to create an e-mail message that states your purpose clearly and succinctly.

Still another advantage to online networking is the opportunity for you to become a known entity in your field. No fear of public speaking need deter you in this effort. You can post an article you have written, contribute to a professional Web site, comment on a blog, and even create your own Web site or blog to promote yourself and your business.

It seems that online networking is perfect for introverts, next generation types, and other quiet networkers. There are advantages for sure, but there are disadvantages and problems to watch out for as well. Don't kid yourself; online networking can be just as hard work as traditional networking. You have the technical issues to deal with as well as acceptance and privacy concerns. The Internet space is not glitch free, so those problems arise all the time.

Then because of the volume of e-mail and the fear of virus infection, spam, and pure junk e-mail, many people filter their e-mails or avoid mail from senders they don't know, or they delete unopened e-mail when the subject line is questionable, dull, or meaningless.

Lastly, online networking is just a tool of networking and should never be considered a replacement for face-to-face contacts. Your primary networking should always be face-to-face, with the Internet, e-mail, postal mail, the telephone, and other communication modes as support channels.

The difference and advantage of face-to-face-networking, especially within membership-based clubs, affiliations, societies, and organizations, can been seen in the way these networked members continue to exert a powerful influence on business, education, politics, entertainment, science, economics, culture, and society in general.

The obvious benefit of joining and participating in face-to-face networking with individuals in these kinds of organizations is that the networking is based on personal friendships, and people are far more willing to help friends in navigating not only through these organizations but also through the areas of the culture in which they have great influence. It is true that the digital social sites are much larger, but they are also much less influenced by personal friendships, connections, trust, reciprocity, and rapport.

Digital networks are weaker links, but they do extend further, even across industry and geographic boundaries, which helps people link up by skill level and talent needs. They also encourage the spread of new ideas at a very rapid pace. The best characteristic of digital social networks is that they are completely inclusive, unlike some of the more traditional face-to-face organizations. Digital networks welcome anyone. However, this benefit also becomes a weakness.

For better or worse, the traditional face-to-face networking encountered through a membership-based organization is generally small enough to create a strong network because most members know each other, thus encouraging favors that will certainly be returned. Digital networks, in contrast, convey a much less loyal connection and therefore would not likely create the environment for as many favors.

People build trusting relationships with others by looking them in the eye, shaking their hand, and getting that "intuitive feeling" about them. As fast and efficient as the Internet is, there is still no substitute for face-to-face contact. With all the time, distance, and technological advantages of online networking, there is one downside that has yet to be overcome: You cannot build rapport and trust online. This chemistry is still done eye-to-eye in the physical presence of another person.

Although we encourage the use of technological tools, they are still just tools to support what you must do primarily in person.

Summary

When networking doesn't come easily, you may develop negative ideas about what it is and your ability to do it. Networking is about creating long-lasting relationships that are mutually beneficial. Anybody and everybody can do it; there is no "correct way" to network. Introverted or quiet people, when they build on their particular strengths, are effective networkers. Develop and follow a process that fits your personality and comfort level, and you will be successful. We like to think of the process as something you can **post** on your bulletin board or on a mirror as a constant reminder. The following list should help remind you:

P= Create a **Plan** that fits your **P**ersonality.

O= **O**wn it in an **Organized** fashion.

S= **S**tick to your own **System**.

T= **T**ake **Time** to build relationships.

Now you have the networking techniques, know the types of people you want to reach for your network, and can develop the characteristics of a good networker. In the next chapter, you will look at how to expand your network.

Endnotes

1. Forrester NACTAS, Q2. 2006. Youth, Media, and Marketing and Financial Online Survey. Cambridge, MA: Forrester Research.

6

How to Expand Your Network

Think of your network as your own ever-evolving web of contacts and resources that you can access for information and links to others. You must first build your network of Web sites. Next, you must learn to get the most out of this network. Finally, you need to keep your web growing, adding new contacts as some drop away and making sure to nurture all the contacts you have worked so hard to make in the first place.

In this chapter, you explore how to build and expand the network you currently have (that's right, you have a current network). It's all about getting the numbers, as you will see. Later, you will consider how to manage and develop the contacts in your network in the most efficient and effective way for you.

The Five Action Steps of Building and Growing Your Network

Recognize you have a network. It includes the people you know and with whom you already have a relationship. What you need to do is incorporate these people into five action steps that will grow and develop your network on an ongoing basis:

1. Identify the people who can help you.

2. Compare this list to a list of people you know who will take your call (see Chapter 3, "Creating Connections: The People You Need in Your Network").

3. Reconnect with those already in your network and keep up the contact as your network grows.

4. Identify the organizations and activities where people you want to know gather.

5. Get involved in these organizations.

Identify the People Who Can Help You

The people who can help you can be specific individuals or the title of an individual within an organization, including your university. If you don't already know the name of the person who currently holds a particular position, find out. Always aim high. The worst that can happen is nothing. The best that can happen is the person in the high position can personally introduce you to the right contact. Of course, in the real world, neither extreme happens as often as something in between, but even something in between is far, far better than doing nothing and getting no help and no contact.

Getting the name of a contact is of vital importance in the interview process, especially if you are going in cold without the help of a network contact. We cannot stress this point strongly enough, but we can say with certainty that dozens, if not hundreds, of your peers (competitors for the jobs you want) will be arriving at the door of the company or organization for which you want to work without a name or title or contact. They will have their freshly printed resumes (usually poorly done) ready to hand to some human resources underling (usually not much older than themselves). Like sheep preparing for a shearing, they will be herded into cubicles for 20-minute courtesy interviews and told, "We'll be in touch if we have anything for you."

If you have a name and title and have set up an interview in advance, you bypass the humiliation of the shearing and useless human resources screening-out process. You have shown initiative, leadership, courage, foresight, problem-solving, and management skills, among other skills, and you are far ahead of your peers and competitors who are circling about looking for their next disappointment. Even if you don't get a job offer, you have made important steps in developing your networking, confidence-building, and interviewing skills. Furthermore, there is a chance the manager you have just met with could turn out to be a network contact.

If the job interview doesn't pan out, you have a perfect opportunity, depending on the person's body language and how much of a personal connection you have made, to ask the person for the names of one or two other contacts he or she could recommend for you to contact based on your skills, abilities, and background. You may also be able to follow up with the interviewer at some point and turn him or her into a networking contact.

Don't prejudge who can help you, how they can help, why they can help, or what they can do for you. Look at networking as a reverse-paranoid would see it, like the whole world is out to do you good!

Compare This List to a List of People You Know Who Will Take Your Call

Go back to the list of people who could possibly be in your network (discussed in Chapter 3). Remember, these people would take your call or return it if you called today. How many of the people you have identified as people who would help you are already in your network? How many may be "six degrees of separation" (or fewer) away from those who can help you? You'll find that some people already in your network have good connections whom you can ask for assistance.

Andrea's friend Jeri knows "everyone." She is a board member of a number of organizations, an active member of her church, and a successful professional business person. She attributes her success to being an active networker herself and to helping others make connections that benefit their careers. She helped Andrea by introducing her to a magazine editor Andrea had identified as someone she wanted to meet. True, Andrea could have called herself and might have gotten through eventually, but her associate Jeri made this connection possible faster and with a more personal touch. Are there more Jeris on your list?

Take another look at the individuals you know—professors, lecturers, university staff members, fellow students, supervisors and bosses, coworkers, and members of organizations to which you belong. Have you stayed in touch? Would a note or phone call be appropriate? What about the alumni of your high school or college? These types of organizations often provide us (Andrea and Michael) with opportunities to develop business in new industries, valuable new contacts that can help us in our professions, and leads for business. Don't forget your neighbors and people who work in your neighborhood. In many cases, these people have seen you grow and develop and would be naturals for you to contact to add to your support network. Some places you can meet include the local coffee shop, the cleaners, the lawn service, or the repair shop. Think of anyone and everyone you and your family has done business with over the years.

Reconnect with Those Already in Your Network and Keep Up the Contact as Your Network Grows

Make a game plan of reconnecting with those people already in your network who can help you. The types of people on the list of those who could be in your network will more than likely take your phone call. Here is an opportunity to reach out. "For what reason?" you ask. No reason. Just to touch base. To say hello. To catch up on what has been happening. To start or restart the networking connection that will be a lifeline perhaps for both of you. Don't be shy; people love calls from friends they haven't heard from in a while, especially if you don't want anything other than to say hello. Imagine the surprise of many old friends who realize the call isn't to ask for anything but just to say hello.

Here is a game plan you can try. We call it the "FOUR-mula for Success." It involves calling and connecting with four people per week from your list:

1. A person you used to work for or do business with but have not been in touch with for a while

2. A person you used to work with

3. A friend you have not seen or spoken to in a while

4. A current friend

Obviously, the fourth call to a current friend will be the easiest and the most fun. It will be your reward for making the other three calls. Work through the list by category. Create a list of people so you have plenty of names in case you come across some numbers that are no longer in service. Keep working from top to bottom, moving to the next type of call only after completing the previous type. Working the telephone involves a rhythm. You need to set aside a block of time in a quiet space and dedicate yourself to the task of making the calls only (no disturbances and no multitasking). You need to start and keep moving through your calling list until you have completed the entire list.

Fitting four completed calls a week into your busy schedule will be relatively easy. This approach breaks down the formidable task of reconnecting with your list into manageable baby steps. It will become a practice you can continue to use as your network grows. Most important will be the results. Imagine how easy it will be to ask for a favor now that you have solidified your relationships with so many people.

Identify the Organizations and Activities Where People You Want to Know Gather

Think of the places, associations, organizations, trade associations, clubs, conferences, events, activities, and other gatherings where people you want to meet gather. Remember the old saying, "If you want blueberries, go to where the blueberries grow."

If you are interested in working in a certain field, you want to select events and activities where people will be gathered to exchange information, make contact, gain more knowledge, or just enjoy the company of others with the same interests.

Make a list. What do you already know about these organizations? Do you belong or know anyone who belongs? Have you ever attended or do you know anyone who has ever attended a meeting? Have you ever read any of the organization's literature? Have you been to the organization's Web site?

The following is a short course on how to identify and locate groups and formats that offer networking opportunities.

Types of Networking Groups

The following four basic types of networking groups are categorized by purpose:

- General networking groups
- Industry-specific groups
- Service groups
- Special-interest groups

Each category has different venues, different networking opportunities, and different values for the individuals attending. You must research the organization and venue, and have an idea of what type of person you expect to meet so you can prepare for the opportunity.

General Networking Groups

General networking groups are those whose stated purpose is to create networking opportunities and allow individuals to exchange leads, contacts, and tips. For the most part, these groups are for general networking and not industry specific. The number of attendees is generally not limited.

Some of the better-known groups include the following:

- Business Network International (BNI): www.bni.com
- Leads Club: www.leadsclub.com

- LeTip International: www.letip.com

- National Association for Female Executives (NAFE): www.nafe.com

- Many local chambers of commerce

These groups generally have regularly scheduled gatherings, usually monthly. The gatherings are not called meetings because there is no official agenda other than networking. The gatherings are frequently held at the same location.

It is important to realize that this process is called networking and not "net-sitting around" or "net-eating and drinking" or "net-dating." The key word is *work*. And as another old saying puts it, "To the victor go the spoils."

A variant of the general networking group is the "strong" or "limited" networking group. These groups generally meet more frequently, up to four times a month, and limit the number of participants from any industry segment to one or two. The meetings are usually more structured, with every participant getting the opportunity to make a brief personal/business presentation. College students would not normally get the chance to attend the strong or limited group events, but if the opportunity arises, you should jump at the chance.

An example of how the strong networking groups work is Business Network International (BNI). This organization is a national organization with chapters in most major U.S. cities. Each chapter has from 10 to 30 members, each from different professions, fields, or industries. There can only be one member from any given field or industry in a chapter—for example, one accountant, one real estate salesperson, one stockbroker. Meetings are typically held early in the morning before the business day begins and last for about an hour. Members get 30 seconds to mention their business and describe the types of clients they hope to find. The idea is that members in the group will become familiar enough with each other's business model that they will refer clients. At each meeting, members report the referrals they have made for their colleagues.

The purpose of this organization is to network and help each other. People who belong to these groups and work hard at helping others get lots of referrals and make lots of beneficial contacts report that they also receive lots of referrals and beneficial contacts. The outcome is like anything else in networking: You get what you give.

Industry-Specific Groups

Industry-specific organizations and groups are created around a specific industry or profession. There are business trade associations (sometimes several) for every major industry group. Some subindustry groups have their own associations. Just about every profession and field has a society or trade group.

The purpose of these organizations is to represent the interests of their particular group in whatever way they can. Some organizations are quite large, active, and powerful, such as the American Association of Advertising Agencies (AAAA), Association of National Advertisers (ANA), Trial Lawyers Association, International Brotherhood of Teamsters, Boy Scouts of America, American Association of Retired Persons (AARP), and American Society of Association Executives (ASAE). These organizations have staffs numbering in the hundreds and annual budgets in excess of $100,000,000.

Networking is not always a major cause supported by these organizations. Nevertheless, the programs the associations do promote, such as educational seminars, conferences, workshops, trade shows, exhibits, panels, and other meetings, are ideal places to network with the industry leaders of the field or industry in which you may want work. Most of the events and activities sponsored by these associations are open to nonmembers, and most have social activities attached to them such as dinners, cocktail hours, breakfasts, pre-meeting get-togethers, and many other opportunities to network.

You can find any trade association by looking at the *Encyclopedia of Associations*. Your college or local library should have a copy. The encyclopedia offers an alphabetized listing of categories and an index. Another search approach is to Google the industry, field, or profession and add the search term "association."

Joining and/or participating in the appropriate trade association for the field or industry you are interested in puts you light years ahead of your peers and competition. The reason is that you will be networking with the very people who will be making the hiring decisions. They will remember and get to know you, which means a boost to your job hunting early in your career, which of course gives you an advantage over your peers who do not engage in this type of networking.

Service Groups

Many public, private, and charitable organizations with members from various walks of life exist to provide public, humane, and social services to others in need.

Examples of some of these types of organizations include the following:

- Rotary International
- Lions Clubs International
- The Benevolent and Protective Order of Elks
- Kiwanis International
- Shriners International
- League of Women Voters
- Women's clubs
- Political clubs
- Student and university clubs
- Gaming clubs
- Church groups
- Parent–teacher associations
- Food pantries
- Shelters for the homeless
- Volunteer organizations
- Veteran assistance clubs
- Veterans' organizations

Whether you belong to any of these groups and use them as a networking venue is dependent on your individual interests and beliefs and how you use your private time. These groups exist to serve the social, community, and civic needs first, not to promote networking.

However, the kinds of people who volunteer and support these organizations are special. Many business and civic leaders donate their time and resources to these causes and take notice of the volunteers who work for these organizations.

If you are like-minded and will benefit by meeting industry and civic leaders who may take notice of your activities, all the better. But you'd better make a real commitment and do the work for the right reasons. Any and all work that you do for these types of groups should be part of the "Experience" section of your resume. Employers are looking for achievements, success in work and assignments, and leadership roles. It does not matter whether you were paid for that kind of experience.

Special-Interest Groups

Special-interest groups are most often overlooked in networking opportunities, yet they can be the most profitable if you keep your eyes and ears open. They are the fun groups and events. Several examples of the types of clubs you could join include your health club or gym, book club, chess club, gaming club, gourmet cooking class, martial arts class, three-on-three basketball, any social get-together.

How do you make connections when the activity is fun? Keep in mind that when you are doing things you like, other people are doing those things because they like to do them too; therefore, you already have something in common. You can join and sign up for fun groups, have fun, and get in some networking at the same time.

Get Involved

The following steps will help you grow your network through involvement with organizations in which people you want to know gather. The first three steps are particularly important and are discussed separately:

1. Go to their meetings and meet the people; then join the organizations that are best for you.

2. Volunteer, join a committee, become active, and go to their social events.

3. Write an article, give a speech or presentation, and do things that get you better known within the group.

4. Sign up for the RSS feed to the group's Web sites or other digital publications. This provides you with an ongoing feed of their thought leadership and visionary ideas.

5. Read their blogs and post your blog comments, or publish your own blog with relevant content.

6. Start to text or e-mail individuals from the organization.

7. Post your own digital content to the organization's Web site.

8. Post your editorials, points of view (POVs), or your thoughts on sites like blip.tv, YouTube, or other video upload sites, or on Twitter.

9. Add content to a wiki site related to the organization's interests.

Go to Meetings and Meet the People; Then Join the Organization(s) Best for You

As you will discover when researching the groups mentioned earlier, there are lots of organizations and activities for profitable networking. The trick is to find the ones best for you.

Most organizations encourage prospective members to attend a couple of meetings before joining. We highly recommend doing so. No matter what you think you already know about an organization, you don't really know it until you have attended and met the members. Use your networking techniques and set a goal to meet at least two new people at each meeting you attend for each prospective organization you are considering joining. Then set a follow-up meeting with each of the people you met to get to know them better and to find out more about the organization.

Be sure to ask if the meetings you attended are typical of most meetings. Find out who generally attends meetings. Sometimes the roster of an organization includes some of the people you would like to meet, but they never attend meetings. Sometimes the meetings are the wrong environment for you to achieve your objectives in your limited time. It is important to pick organizations that are best for your needs.

You may want to consider the "2–2–2 strategy":

- Attend **two** meetings.

- Meet **two** people and exchange **two** business cards.

- Arrange for **two** follow-up meetings.

This strategy will help you find out whether you want to join the organization and will also expand your network by at least two people.

Another approach to take with an organization you are considering joining is to ask to see a list of past and future programs. Examine these for content and speakers. This information will help tell you whether the organization is of interest to you. Are the speakers people you want to hear and meet? Are there other programs, activities, and workshops offered that would be of interest and/or help to you? Does the organization offer a newsletter? Web site? Job postings? Is there some way you could contribute? Is the organization network friendly? Can you benefit as well as share?

Volunteer, Join a Committee, Become Active

Michael spent 20 years in nonprofit membership organizations primarily in membership marketing. In that time, he conducted many membership satisfaction studies as well as studied the results of dozens of other membership satisfaction studies. There is one common and repeating theme in all that data: Active participating members get more benefit from membership organizations than members who are not active. Furthermore, they don't get just a little more benefit; they get significantly more benefit. In many cases, they report getting returns on their investments in multiples of the money and time they spent.

As a side benefit from volunteering, over and above the intrinsic feelings of reward for helping others, you can add the volunteer experience to your resume. Employers sometimes view volunteer experience and the applicant's experience and achievements with great interest. Volunteering demonstrates initiative, drive, empathy, concern for others, teamwork, leadership, organizational skills, motivation, and other soft skills that are in high demand in the workforce.

It has been said before, and it is worth saying again:

> *Networking is hard work, but it pays off. If you network, you will be significantly ahead of your peers and classmates who do not network in terms of career and social capital.*

When you become involved, you will meet more people, make more contacts, get to know the organization better, and expand your network faster. Here are some ways to do this:

- **Volunteer to be a greeter.** When people are registering for a meeting or event, a greeter welcomes them. Working as a greeter is a great way to meet a lot of people. The greeter meets everyone who attends, so you will be sure to have introduced yourself to everyone attending, including those whom you wanted to meet. You will then have an "opening line" to connect with them the next time you meet.

- **Join a committee.** If you just attend meetings, you will limit your ability to meet and get to know members of the organization. After all, the majority of the time spent at a meeting is devoted to the agenda and program content. Your objective is to expand your network, not just listen to a speaker, even a great one. If you volunteer for a committee or a project that interests you, you will be introduced to a number of other people.

A committee for which to volunteer in an organization is the program committee—one of the most interesting and profitable. As an active member of this committee, you usually get to meet and interact with all the speakers and thought leaders in the field as well as the other committee members and most likely the organizational officers and directors.

Write an Article, Give a Speech, Become Known

Remember, before you joined, you checked out the organization's roster, newsletter, list of programs, and Web site, and you thought about whether you could make a contribution. Now that you have had a chance to learn about the types of articles that are published in the newsletter or on the Web site, it is time to make a contribution. Write an article and submit it to the editor or webmaster. Even if you volunteer to write a recap of a recent meeting, you will get a byline and a publishing credit. You will become known. Meeting people will become easier when they remember you wrote an article, or you can remind them that you wrote an article. In either case, you will have made a contribution to the organization.

Another way to become known and therefore meet people is to give a speech or presentation for an organization. Groups are always looking for programs and breakout sessions for larger meetings or conventions. Take the opportunity to become a presenter.

If you are fearful of public speaking, take a course in presentation skills and sharpen and practice these skills because they are critical to your career success. A presentation can be as simple as teaching a basic class in a topic you know a lot about.

Summary

What you have seen in this chapter is that to expand your network, you must create the opportunities to keep it growing and identify the people you want to meet and know. Examine your existing network and reconnect with those people with whom you have been out of touch. Then keep it up. Maintaining these contacts is as simple as making four phone calls a week.

Look for the places you are likely to find the people you want to meet. Research and join organizations where they might gather. Don't limit yourself just to networking groups and industry organizations. Think about community service and special-interest groups as well. Become active in these organizations and become known. The following list reviews the five action steps for building and growing your network:

1. Identify the people who can help you.

2. Compare this list to the list you started in Chapter 3, those people you know will take your call.

3. Reconnect with those already in your network and keep up the contact as your network grows.

4. Identify the organizations and activities where people you want to know gather.

5 Get involved in these organizations.

The more people who know who you are, the more people you have the opportunity to meet. Soon you will have a large list of contacts who will not only take your phone call, but who will be glad to hear from you and glad to help you.

To keep these contacts requires time, attention, and follow-up. In the next chapter, you will learn how to nurture these contacts, creating connections that last a lifetime.

7

Keeping Your Network Alive and Growing

After you have been networking for a while, you will conquer your fears and develop more confidence. You will be able to walk into rooms full of strangers (networking gold mines) with a goal of meeting and following up with at least two new people, and this strategy will work. Congratulate yourself.

You will see the stack of business cards you have collected growing, and you will be the proud owner of a large and growing database of contacts—people who will take your phone calls, return your e-mails, and do favors for you. Now you have to figure out how to keep it all going.

How, you wonder, do I keep in touch with these contacts and nurture the relationships I have started? In this chapter, you examine how to keep in touch with those in your network and build long-lasting, mutually beneficial relationships.

As in any relationship, the first thing you should do is get to know the other person's interests, family, school activities, and important events. Then you need to find ways to keep in touch. Doing so includes writing the important, effective thank-you note. One of the most effective ways to stay in touch is to become a resource to others.

Finally, we address the issue of how to make sure you regularly touch base with everyone in your networking database.

Getting to Know You

All relationships begin with a "getting to know you" phase. The handshake, the chat, the sizing each other up. Why are meetings like this important and relevant? Networks must first be formed with an initial meeting. Most relationships endure because you continue to stay in touch after the initial face-to-face meeting.

Remember the list of contacts you made who would probably take your phone call? Why would they take your call? A contact you've previously met would take your call because you have a relationship that was built on a first meeting that continued to develop and because these people saw some reciprocal opportunity in the relationship, some mutual benefit. Getting to know a contact gives you information you can use to stay in touch so that everyone in your network can become a contact for life.

Find Out the Best Way to Stay in Touch

When you meet someone you want to stay in contact with, one of the first things you should ask is, "What is the best way for us to keep in touch?" Everyone has a preferred way to communicate. Don't assume that because your classmates use text and e-mail, these are the preferred methods. Some people still prefer the telephone.

Even if they can't take a call, voice mail works for them. For these people, a series of voice-mail messages may be perfectly suitable. Other people prefer e-mail and are good at responding quickly, as you should be. Many younger people respond primarily by text and not by phone. Whatever the preference, you need to know so that your communications are as efficient as possible. You should record this kind of information in your contact database.

Note Important Dates, Birthdates, and Anniversaries

Find out important dates and events, birthdates, anniversaries, and other important occasions. Knowing such details provides an opportunity to get in touch with a card, e-mail, text, or phone call.

Andrea always asks about birthdays—not necessarily the year (that could be problematic), but the month and day, or even the person's astrological sign. She records this information in her contact database. Then each month she sends out an appropriate birthday reminder—cards for some, e-mails and phone calls for others.

The fact that you remember is the important thing. Anniversaries, birthdays, and special dates are opportunities for you to reconnect and be in touch. Be alert to what people mention about these dates. Some people are proud of certain anniversaries and the fact that you remembered will help the relationship grow.

Learn About Families, Interests, and Hobbies

Ask your network contacts about their families, interests, and hobbies. This kind of information gives you conversation starters (people love to talk about themselves). It also provides you with information that helps you to stay in touch. Finally, this kind of information can provide you with ideas that can make you a resource for others and turn you into a strong contact.

Keeping in Touch and Showing Appreciation

When you are armed with information, you can use the following ways to keep in touch and help build your relationships.

Use Handwritten Notes

The art of writing handwritten notes, especially in college, is sadly disappearing. The U.S. Postal Service reports that only 4 percent of mail is personal correspondence. However, this mode of communication is your key to success. What have you learned in your marketing and communications classes?

Differentiation is how you stand out and get noticed. If you write handwritten notes, we guarantee they will be noticed and read. Think about it. When you open your mailbox, doesn't a handwritten envelope stand out among all the other mail, and don't you read it first? And doesn't the thought cross your mind, "Someone is thinking of me"? A personal note is the most effective way to connect and reconnect with others and make them feel good about knowing you.

Write Thank-You Notes

One of the very best and least expensive public relations tools you can use is the simple thank-you note. As discussed in Chapter 4, "Characteristics of Great Networkers," you can never say thank you too many times as long as you are sincere.

Here are eight reasons to send a thank-you note:

- For time and consideration given to you
- For being interviewed for a job
- For a compliment you have received
- For a piece of advice you have received
- For business you have received
- For a referral you have been given
- For a gift someone has given you
- For help someone has given you

It makes good sense to have note cards and stamps close by so that when you have some "found time," you can write a note or two and drop them in the mail.

Now there is software available online that generates note cards with your personal message in a handwriting font; thus, the note appears handwritten even though you have typed it on your computer. You simply print it, put a stamp on it, and mail it. Check Andrea's Web site (www.selfmarketing.com) for more information on this service, which she uses herself.

Send Other Notes

Besides the thank-you note, you can send several other types of notes anytime to stay in touch and be helpful:

- **FYI (for your information).** You can send articles, clippings, or URLs that may be of interest to people in your network. These notes can be related to the recipient's business, college courses, family, hobbies, personal interests, or something you think he or she might be interested in. Include a brief note, such as "I thought of you when I came across this and thought you might [enjoy it, find it useful, be interested in it, want it for your files, etc.]."

- **Congratulations.** Send one of these notes for a new job, a promotion, an award, an honor, or any event for which your network contact received recognition. This is a perfect opportunity to stay in touch.

- **Nice talking with you.** Both of us send these notes after a phone conversation (especially a phone appointment or conference call), a meeting, a chance encounter and conversation, and always after meeting someone new at an event.

- **Thinking of you.** These notes are sent for no particular reason other than to stay in touch. They are easy to use because you can buy a card with this sentiment and just add a brief note.

Send Holiday Notes

Andrea sends holiday greetings to everyone in her network contact list and uses other occasions to remember and stay in touch as well. Think about your network contacts. Could you send Thanksgiving, Easter, St. Patrick's Day, Friendship Week, Mother's Day, or Father's Day cards? The calendar is full of special day opportunities you can use to stay in touch.

Use "The Power of Three" Note Plan

You may be thinking, "This is a lot of notes and cards! Who has the time?" Here is a technique Andrea adopted and has used successfully for years. It is easy and does not take much time from your busy day. Moreover, we can say from experience that you can be sure it will pay off in building solid networking relationships. Every day, send three hand-written notes. Make them short notes to express any of the messages we have discussed. You can send these notes to the following people:

- Fellow students
- Former coworkers
- Friends
- Family members
- Club and association members
- Former teachers
- Prospective contacts
- Customers

If you write and send just three notes a day, by the end of the work-week, you will have contacted 15 people, and by the end of the year, 750 people. Writing these notes should not take more than ten minutes a day. You can write them first thing in the morning before classes, during lunch, after your classes end, whenever works best for your schedule. Writing notes is easy when you get in the habit. Your notes do not have to be perfectly crafted; it is the thought that counts.

After you get the hang of this technique, add in a multiplier, and a total of:

- Three extra notes
- Three extra e-mails
- Three extra phone calls

That is 2,250 connections in a year!

Take Full Advantage of E-Mail

The handwritten note is special; however, in today's world, we are fortunate to have a way to be in instant contact with so many people all around the world. In fact, there is very little excuse for not showing appreciation or following up in a timely fashion with e-mail.

It is perfectly appropriate to send a thank-you note for any of the eight reasons mentioned earlier via e-mail. It is also fine to send an article of interest as an e-mail attachment. Just be careful and do not bombard your network contacts with articles, notes, or (shudder) chain letters that are making the rounds on the Internet.

Remember, you are extending a professional courtesy, and the message should be tailored to the recipient, not a mass mailing. Make sure you have a valid reason to send the information, and always include a personal note. You will consider networking etiquette in the next chapter, but for now remember to follow one fast rule about e-mail correspondence: Always reply to e-mails within 48 hours of receipt. Not responding quickly makes you appear uninterested and even rude.

While we may have the urge to send an instant follow-up thank-you message by text, the speed of the thank you isn't the point. The thoughtfulness and the time spent writing a handwritten note is the point. So forgo the technological advantage of speed for the humanistic benefit of character.

Send Gifts to Show Your Appreciation

Sometimes showing your appreciation with a gift is appropriate. Sending a gift sets you apart. When is it appropriate to send a gift? Andrea often sends a gift after she completes a project, when someone gets promoted, for a birthday or holiday, or when someone has done her a special favor.

In business and academic situations, you need to be careful about the nature of the gift. Keep in mind that this is a gesture of appreciation and you do not want to place the recipient in the awkward position of having to turn down your gift due to company or school policy. In general, food is the best kind of gift in this situation. Most businesses or universities that do not allow gifts to employees and professors allow a gift of food that can be shared with all. Some good choices include a fruit basket, a popcorn tin, or a box of candy or other edible goodies.

Follow-Ups: The Key to Keeping Your Network Alive and Growing

You could be the master of working a room and leave each networking event with a pocketful of business cards, but if you do not follow up with these people and others already in your network, you will never be successful at networking. Follow-up is the key.

There are four absolute must-follow-up situations. When you follow up in these situations and in the time suggested, you will be successful at creating and maintaining an active list of contacts who trust and respect you and who will gladly help you out when you find the need to ask. Here are the situations and ways to follow up:

1. Within 24 hours after a meeting, send a note or e-mail, or call by phone, to say any of the following, depending on the circumstances of your meeting:

   - "How nice to meet you."

   - "Thank you for your time and consideration."

   - "We should meet again."

   - "Thank you for the useful information."

   This type of follow-up not only is a courtesy, but also differentiates you from the myriad of others the person may have met.

2. If you have promised to send materials, to set up a meeting, or to pass on a referral, keep your word and do it within the time promised or sooner. Making these promises at a meeting or event is easy, but it is the person who follows up in a timely manner who is remembered and trusted.

3. Call within two weeks after having made a suggestion to get together, whether over a meal or at a more formal meeting. Just saying "Let's do lunch" is not an effective networking technique. Don't suggest getting together unless you mean it; then follow up to set a specific date and place. Twenty-four hours before your

get-together, call again to confirm. When you follow up in this manner, you will be perceived as being sincere and professional.

4. If a contact gives you a referral or passes your resume on to help you out, be sure to thank your contact and let him or her know the results. You should also do this for any tangible advice given to you from a network contact. People who offer help to you in whatever form deserve to know the results of their advice. More importantly, they absolutely deserve a thank you.

Following up not only shows good communication skills but also builds solid relationships for the future and shows respect for others. It helps people remember you and makes them more willing to continue helping you.

Becoming a Resource for Others

Share your skills and experience, happy in the knowledge that you are helping friends and fellow students and colleagues. Other people appreciate and seek out knowledgeable individuals who give generously of their expertise. When you have been a resource to others, people are more willing to help you when you ask.

Andrea had a client named Joan who was a good example of this. Joan always went out of her way to help others. When people needed something, they called on Joan. It was no surprise that when Joan lost her job in a corporate downsizing a few years ago, she only had to make a few calls to some close network contacts and she was back to work in no time with a better and more prestigious position. It was easy for her to ask for help because she had consistently been so helpful to so many others.

Managing Face-to-Face Time

Spending time with someone in person is always more powerful, effective, and memorable than carrying on a conversation by phone, text, or e-mail. The reason for this is what we call "chemistry." Sociologists call it "rapport," but many people just refer to it as "connecting."

You know the feeling—the energy and excitement you feel when you have made a strong bond with someone over common interests or issues. This rapport can be made and felt only when you are in the other person's physical presence and can look into his or her eyes. The bond of rapport can lead to a colleague, a friend, and certainly a strong network contact.

People love doing things for and with other people they know and like. This phenomenon has positive health benefits. Making network contacts actually helps strengthen a positive mental outlook for people.

In today's busy world, it is increasingly difficult to find the time to make face-to-face contacts. Distance is also a limiting factor. However, as with many other things, if you make a plan, you are much more likely to carry out the activity. So make a plan to spend some time in face-to-face contact with certain network contacts. Because face-to-face meetings require more planning, plan them at least 30 to 60 days in advance. You have to be both persistent and creative to make sure you get this face time.

Besides traditional meetings such as breakfast, lunch, dinner, and after-work outings, suggest meeting for coffee or tennis or golf, or meet at a museum or at an industry or academic meeting. Think creatively. Everybody is busy and appreciates new and unique suggestions. Be persistent; face-to-face meetings are invaluable in building solid networking relationships.

Keeping in Touch with Everyone in Your Growing Network

As your network continues to grow, you will want to have a system to stay in touch with each of your network contacts. We are frequently asked how we keep in touch with several thousand people on each of our networking lists. Here is how we do it: Divide the list into three categories—A, B, and C. There is a contact plan for each category.

The C list is made up of "touch-base" people. These are casual acquaintances—interesting people we have met and with whom we would like to stay in touch, and with whom there is no immediate personal involvement or business connection. Each person gets a quarterly contact of some sort. Andrea sends a quarterly newsletter. Michael sends an

"Update Note" or a short interesting article with a note such as "Have you seen this?" Holiday cards are appropriate.

The B list is made up of "associates." These people are those with whom we are actively involved, either professionally or personally. We find ways to meet each of these individuals in person, for a meal, coffee, tea, snack, or a chat at least two times a year. In addition, we send them up to six personal notes a year. We call them every other month just to say hello. We also give these individuals holiday cards and gifts, and Andrea sends her B list her newsletter.

The A list is made up of "close friends and associates." We see these individuals in person at least four times a year. We frequently give them special gifts and contact them with personal notes and calls. We send these individuals articles of interest as well as newsletters and holiday cards.

The A, B, and C lists are not static, and the rules are not forged in stone. This system represents a plan and provides a road map for how to manage a contact list effectively. The following list will help you remember how to make F.A.C.E. contact work for you:

> **F** = Make it **Fun. Find** unique things to do and places to meet.
>
> **A** = **Adapt** to each other's timetables and surroundings.
>
> **C** = **Connect** and find common interests.
>
> **E** = Know when to **Exit**; be respectful of each other's time.

Summary

In this chapter, you explored how to keep your network alive and growing. You have to nurture and tend to your network much the way a gardener tends to his or her garden. First, you plant seeds, then water and feed the growing plants, and then, hopefully, they will blossom. For your network, first you make the contact; then you follow up, become a resource, stay in touch; and then, hopefully, you create relationships that grow and are mutually beneficial. Your network, just like a garden, will grow and prosper only if you take the time to tend to it carefully.

As in any social business discourse, you should observe rules of etiquette and conventional behavior. Sadly, in today's world, driven by short-term results, many of these rules and conventions are ignored, and the result is "negative networking." Not only is it rude, it just doesn't work. The next chapter reviews these rules of etiquette and offers some examples of how to avoid negative networking.

8

Networking Etiquette

What would you think if you were at a wedding reception and a guest seated across from you began handing out business cards? At first, you might just think the person was outgoing and friendly, but what would you think if this guest then began asking people at the table questions about their personal investments? Worse, what if this bore began bragging about how he could do better than you were doing now regardless of your situation? Still worse, what if this embarrassment of a so-called networker called everyone at the table and asked for a meeting and referrals?

Obviously, this is an example of a networking disaster, and an actual event that happened to Andrea. This behavior was truly poor networking etiquette—"negative networking," as we call it.

Networking is all about establishing positive relationships and building trust and reciprocity. In our example, the man started working on those at the table before the soup was served. Not only did he not bother to get to know the people at the table, but he also showed poor manners and lack of common courtesy.

Etiquette is just plain good manners, common courtesy. Successful business relationships, just like successful personal relationships, rely on common courtesy. In this chapter, you look at some rules of etiquette that relate to networking activities, but you should remember and observe them in any business or social situation.

You probably learned the basic rules of etiquette as you grew up—from your parents, school peers, mentors, and professors, and sometimes by observation. Here, we describe some common networking situations and rules for the proper etiquette for each.

Networking Events, Meetings, or Activities

Following are some tips to follow when you attend networking events, meetings, or activities:

- Arrive on time, or better yet, early. Arriving late shows disrespect and is a red flag of poor character. It signals you think your time is more important and valuable than those at the meeting. Early arrival demonstrates enthusiasm and respect for people's time. Furthermore, an early arrival gives you time to settle in and further plan your activities.

- Place your name tag on the right side and as high as appropriate on your garment. This places it in a direct line of eye contact with people you will meet and helps people see and remember your name.

- Exchange business cards with ease. Place several loose cards in your shirt, blouse, or jacket pocket or in a spot where you can reach them easily without digging or rummaging through your pants pockets, purse, or wallet. Make sure your business cards are fresh.

- Do not walk around with a stack of resumes, and do not just hand out your resumes to everyone you meet. Keep your resumes in a folder or briefcase until it becomes obvious you need them.

- Make eye contact with each person you are about to meet. Looking someone in the eye shows respect and that you are honest and trustworthy. Eye contact is a nonverbal body language sign of trustworthiness and honesty. However, there is a flip side of too much of a good thing. Although making eye contact is important, it is equally important to break off eye contact briefly after about eight to ten seconds before regaining eye contact again. Too much eye contact is creepy and unnerving and makes others feel unnecessarily uncomfortable—not what you want to accomplish—so avoid staring.

- Shake hands (if appropriate) firmly. There is nothing worse than a cold, loose grip. On the other hand, no death grips either. This is not a contest to prove your strength. Be cautious of the over-the-top grip because this is body language for power, and unless you are the most powerful person in the room, it is inappropriate. Also, avoid the two-handed shake where you grab the other person by the shoulder or arm and shake his or her hand. This handshake is way too personal and also a power gesture you need to avoid in this situation.

- Be aware of the difference between business, social, and personal space.

  Business space is five or more feet apart and conveys proper business distance.

  Social space is between two and four feet and conveys a warmer, friendlier feeling in which you can discuss almost any topic.

  Personal space is closer than two feet and causes many people discomfort unless they invite you into their space by shaking your hand with a double-grasp, pulling you in, placing a hand on shoulder, or otherwise moving to close the space.

- Welcome others into your conversation with grace and a smile. Extend your hand(s), welcome, and be inclusive.

- Don't eat and carry on a conversation. Do one or the other, but not both at the same time.

- If you drink and carry on a conversation, either use little or no ice, or wrap napkins around the glass. A cold glass leads to a cold handshake.

Meals at Large Events or Private Functions

Here are some tips to follow when you attend meals at large events or private functions:

- Turn off your cell phone or mobile device. Answering—or worse yet, making—a call at such an event shows disrespect. It says the people at the event are not important.

- First introduce yourself to the person seated on your right and then your left. Then introduce yourself to the rest of the table. As others join the table, introduce yourself and others to them.

- Wait for those at the head table to begin eating, or if at a private meal, wait for the host or hostess to begin. If you are the host or hostess, you must begin.

- When ordering, allow your guest to order first. Direct the server first to your guest and then you. Then select your entrée accordingly. It is safest to pick something in the mid-price range.

- If you don't know which utensil to use, working from the outside in is always a safe start. Alternatively, watch the host or hostess.

- Keep your napkin on your lap until you leave the event. If you leave the table, temporarily place the napkin on your chair. After you finish your meal, place the napkin next to your plate.

- Water glasses and salad plates work this way: Liquids on the right, solids on the left.

- When you finish, place your knife and fork in a parallel position across the center of your plate.

- Even if you are still hungry, stop eating if everyone else at the table is done.

- Don't talk with your mouth full. (Also, don't talk with your mind empty.)

- Hold off talking about business until the main course is cleared. This allows ample time for making small talk and getting acquainted. In addition, the servers will be out of the way.

- Ask before you take notes. It is perfectly acceptable to take notes at a business networking event, but first ask out of courtesy. Use a small notepad or index cards, not a full-sized notebook or a laptop.

Making Introductions

In the business world, when introducing two people, defer to position and age. Gender is not a factor. Try to include something that the individuals might have in common. An introduction is normally made in a logical order:

- **Younger to older.** For example: "Mr. President, I would like to introduce my daughter Sue, the president of her eighth-grade class."

- **Your company peer to a peer in another company.** For example: "John, since we have not yet worked on projects together, this is someone I wanted you to meet and someone with whom I worked previously on many projects, Linda Jones."

- **Junior executive to senior executive.** For example: "Joan Roberts, Manager of Logistics, please meet our CEO Susan White, whom I believe got her start in business in logistics."

- **Fellow executive to client.** For example: "Robert, I would like to introduce you to the Purchasing Manager of XYZ Company, Joe Smith."

- **Personal contact to business contact.** For example: "Maria is a friend of mine, and I have wanted her to meet someone who knows as much about accounting as she does. Maria, this is Don."

Understanding E-Mail, Texting, and Phone Etiquette

Technology is both an aid and an obstacle to helping bringing people together in networking situations. Some studies have shown mobile devices, cell phones, and tablets have increased breaches in workplace and social etiquette by more than double in just a few years. Think about how many times you have sat down to a meal with family or friends and out came the cell phones or mobile devices. Like any tool, when used properly, they enhance our lives, but when they are misused, well, you are smart enough to know the impression you'll leave.

E-Mail Etiquette

E-mail and texting make our lives easier. They are immediate, efficient, and convenient. They are wonderful communications tools; however, sometimes your messages can be misunderstood if you do not follow certain conventions. You may be accustomed to using a unique language and relaxed rules for spelling and grammar online. However, keep this point in mind:

> **Digital messages are forever. Any digital message or signal that you send stays in cyberspace forever. You can delete it from your computer, but after it is sent, someplace, sometime, any message could be recalled by somebody. After you hit the Send button, the message is no longer yours. It belongs to whoever has possession of it.**

Also bear in mind, e-mail and texting lack the vocal inflections required to express tone, regardless of the icons, tags, and other devices that attempt to convey emotions and feelings. You can't digitize body language—yet.

Here are some general digital communications etiquette tips:

- Keep digital communications brief, to the point, and focused.
- Use meaningful, thoughtful subject lines.
- Use a format: purpose, body, and action.
- If you need to send a long document, send it as an attachment.

- Do not forward jokes, chain letters, flame letters, junk e-mail, or other instant messages.

- Never e-mail when you are angry or emotional, or when your judgment is clouded. Better to wait a few hours or a day.

- Always reread your message before clicking the Send button. *Make sure you are saying what you want to say.*

- Answer all e-mails within 48 hours.

Texting Etiquette

As just mentioned, texting is certainly one of our most popular forms of communication, yet there is etiquette to it, especially when you realize that in networking, everything you do conveys a message. Speed plus convenience make texting often the most popular "on the go" conversation. In fact, more than five billion text messages are sent daily.

Keep these pointers in mind:

- Keep it brief. A text message should be two to three sentences at most. Less is more. Get to the point and save the long passages for a real conversation. Think of texts as preludes or follow-ups to conversation, not the conversation itself. Keep them short. Typing more than 160 characters means that making a phone call or sending e-mail is the better way to deliver your message.

- Don't be a text pest and assume that people will receive your message right after you send it. You will turn into a persistent texter, and that is rude.

- Do text to confirm plans so that the recipient can reply with a simple yes or no. If there is a change in venue, opt for a real call or e-mail. Also, be careful of the tone your text may convey. Again, this is another reason to be brief and to the point.

- Do use proper grammar and punctuation, especially with a new networking contact. Be careful also of using abbreviations and the slang associated with texts.

- Don't send many, if any, attachments via text; they will clog the recipient's inbox, preventing him or her from receiving other messages. Texting is not the place for volume.

- Do text at the right time. Don't text when you are in a meeting or at a meal; doing so is distracting to others and rude. Also, do not send any communication, especially a text, when your judgment may be impaired or you haven't had enough sleep. Definitely never text while driving; this point seems obvious because texting and driving can be deadly.

- You should always reread your text before hitting the Send button. Taking the few seconds to reread can save you from a lifetime of embarrassment.

- As in e-mail and clicking Reply All, be careful to verify whom you are sending the text to.

- Never text while another person is speaking; it is rude.

- Texting a thank-you note is *not okay*. Instead, call, send an e-mail, or even better, send a handwritten note.

- Don't leave people guessing who you are. They may not have your contact information in their phones. Identify yourself.

- Never send texts or e-mails that go to a smart phone after bedtime. If the recipient forgot to turn his or her phone to silent, the beep will wake up that person at 3:00 a.m. That's not a great impression to leave a networking contact...or a friend for that matter.

- Never text or use your mobile device while talking to another person. You will come across to that person and to others watching you as distracted and disrespectful.

- Don't think you can multitask. Multitasking is a myth.

Phone Etiquette

Here are some general phone etiquette tips:

- Return all phone calls within 48 hours, even if you don't have an answer yet. Let your caller know you are working on the issue.

- When making a phone call, ask the person if this is a good time to talk; if not, ask when a good time is and follow the other person's lead.

- State the purpose of your call and indicate that you would like a few minutes of the person's time. Don't take any longer unless the other person insists.

- When leaving a message, clearly and succinctly state your name, purpose of the call, and action you need. Most importantly, when leaving your number, speak slowly and clearly.

- Don't leave long voice mails. Get to the point quickly and try to hold your message to less than 30 seconds.

- When calling a contact referral, state your name and who referred you. For example, "Hello, my name is Michael Faulkner. Andrea Nierenberg suggested I give you a call to ask if you would be kind enough to tell me about how you have been so successful in launching a new product during this recession. Is this a good time to talk?"

- Smile when you are talking. The other person can't see you, but he or she can tell in your voice whether or not you are smiling.

- Don't work on other tasks while on the phone. People can tell when you are trying to do several things at once. It is rude and disrespectful.

- Don't put the other person on speakerphone unless doing so is absolutely unavoidable or the person requests it.

- When answering, try this: "Hello, this is _____. How may I help you [or how may I be of service]?" Cutting down on unnecessary chit-chat saves 1–2 minutes per call, and if you answer 20 calls a day, that saves you nearly 40 minutes!

Knowing the Right Way to Ask for a Favor

When you have been a good resource to others, asking for a favor is easy. Most people are happy to help, especially if you know how to ask. Here are some opening lines you could use:

- "Perhaps you could help me...."

- "Who do you know that...?"

- "Would you feel comfortable referring me to _____?"

- "I would really appreciate your help on...."

- "I'd like to get your advice on...."

- "Maybe you could steer me in the right direction."

- "If you were in my shoes, what would you do?"

- "How would you handle this?"

- "There is something that I could really use your expert advice with."

- "It would be wonderful if I could get your opinion (or advice) on something. Would you consider helping me?"

Always remember to say thank you and follow up with an e-mail, handwritten thank-you note, phone call, and a gift, if appropriate.

Following Up

Following up is always good networking etiquette:

- Always send a thank-you note or an e-mail within 48 hours after a meeting. Thank your contact for his or her time and consideration, and confirm any follow-up steps.

- Get permission for any "next steps." Ask when would be a good time to call or get together. Also ask, "What is the best way for us to keep in touch?" The person may prefer a text, e-mail, telephone, letter, or a face-to-face meeting. These steps show respect for the other person's time and preference.

- Be sure to follow up when asked specific questions. When asked specifically for a referral, materials, data, your resume, or other source material or information, ask, "When do you need this?" And then send it on time—or earlier.

Networking at a Non-Networking Event

Networking, if you think of it as connecting, learning about and helping others, and building relationships, can be done anywhere, anytime. However, remember how inappropriate the stockbroker acted at the wedding (at the beginning of this chapter)? Had he been at a meeting specifically for networking, his actions might have been marginally more appropriate. The purpose of a networking meeting is to share personal information and ask for referrals.

The purpose of a wedding reception, dinner, party, or many other social events is to celebrate. Does this mean you should not meet people at such functions and not begin to establish relationships? Of course not. However, the proper way to do this at social events and other non-networking events is to use discretion. Follow these rules and you won't get into trouble:

- Recognize where you are, the purpose of the event, and why you are there.

- When you come across a potential network contact, graciously suggest that perhaps this is not the best time to discuss business/networking opportunities and suggest a call for a later date. Offer some options. This is a perfect example of why you need business cards.

- Ask permission before exchanging business cards or personal information. Then the exchange should be as discreet as handing a tip to a maître d'.

- Recognize that in several types of establishments, such as private clubs, conducting business is simply not allowed. Be aware of where you are and follow the prescribed behavior.

Keeping Score

For some people, networking means that they do someone a favor and a favor is owed to them in return. It is almost as if they keep a scorecard for every contact. Both of us just believe in helping others, and if we receive something in return, we consider it a gift, not a right or a privilege. Here are some guidelines on "keeping score":

- Always return a favor given to you.

- Don't expect or demand that a favor be returned to you.

- Give only for the sake of giving.

- Under promise and over deliver.

Understanding Networking Competition

There is another point you should consider about competition and networking: Some people, by their nature, are very competitive. Although there is nothing inherently wrong with "keeping score" and trying to be the best networker possible, you need to be cautious about turning your networking into a competition just to win or to build up the largest number of contacts, or to be the first in your graduating class to get a job or a promotion using networking. Networking is a professional experience. Using it to keep pace with your classmates or to rack up numbers of contacts, or solely as a means to an end, is a misuse of the purpose of networking.

Summary

This chapter stressed the importance of etiquette in networking. It is important to recognize that networking and good manners are compatible. Networking is about building relationships with others, and as in any relationship, common courtesy counts.

Are you wondering how to keep track of all the contacts and information you are gathering as you master the networking process? In the next chapter, you will examine how to organize and keep track of thousands of contacts.

9

The Social Media

Someone said, nothing is new, everything is just repackaged old ideas. There are a lot of baby boomers and seniors looking at what we call social media, and most might disagree—to many of them, social media looks pretty unreal. It can seem intimidating if you let the buzz words, technological lingo, and hype get in the way of what is going on, but really it's sociable communications—something humans have been doing for hundreds of years.

What Is Social Media?

Social media is the online environment created for the purpose of instant interactive communication and mass collaboration. It is the old camp fire, the nineteenth-century family dinner table, the Sunday afternoon church social, and the neighbors gathering at the backyard fence all rolled into one and magnified by some exponentially large number.

Social media is the place where interactive communication and mass collaboration occurs. A set of digital and electronic communications software and various digital technologies allow individuals and organizations to connect and collaborate and vote and see and talk and otherwise be transparent with each other.

What makes social media different from anything man has done up to this point is the fundamental change in the form of human communications. We can now instantly communicate with one other person or millions of people in seconds through a variety of media using words, pictures, graphics, or code. Literally any way that digital content can be communicated from one to others is within our capabilities. Social media, in this context, is about communities of individuals, bound by a shared interest or purpose, who have come together through a variety of digital communications channels such as Facebook, Pinterest, YouTube, LinkedIn, Twitter, Digg, Meet-Up, Google+, Deviant Art, Live Journal, Tagged, Café Mom, Ask.fm, personal blogs, and wireless devices. The value of social media to support personal networking is found in the collaboration of multiple communities, on a massive scale, simultaneously leveraging the knowledge, experience, background, thought leadership, intuition, research, and ideas of many people on a variety of issues, problems, opportunities, and solutions. The benefits of the diversity of heterogeneous thinking (the wisdom of the crowd) all add to the value of a vast network expanding the value chain of individuals.

The Functioning of the Parts Is Determined by the Nature of Social Media

The behavior of social media is determined by the purposeful configuration and functioning of these individual elements: (1) strategy, (2) technology, and (3) audience. These three components are so unified as a whole entity that social media cannot be effectively described nor can it achieve its complete purpose simply by attempting to make the parts operate independently.

Wikis, social networking sites, blogs, video posts, peer-to-peer sharing, hash tags, e-mail, instant messaging, cloud storage, bookmarking, share this, threaded discussions, idea engines, answer market places, prediction markets, virtual second worlds, and avatars are just the current, usable, and acceptable technologies. They are just the current communication tools and channels and are not critical per se. They are but parts of the whole phenomena of social media and have a use, but without the strategic purpose or the mission of interactive communications and mass collaboration providing a strategic gestalt, they are just individual technological game pieces.

The audiences for social media, by the nature of their demographic and psychographic characteristics, seek to organize and apply the technologies and parts of social media into the phenomenon that reconnects individuals and rejects the previous sociological trends of our culture toward atomism and the collapse of community that Robert Putnam described in his 2000 classic study, *Bowling Alone.*

Putnam gave us a picture of the negative changes that were occurring in American culture as a result of our love affair with electronic entertainment devices. The changes focused on our loss of face-to-face networking and community building. Putnam told stories of this loss, including how we now bowl alone instead of in leagues or with friends.

Who Uses Social Media?

The two major audiences for which social media can provide far-reaching benefits are individuals and organizations. The first group, consisting of individuals, is the only audience that we address in this book.

Individuals have the potential to use social media to dramatically expand into communities of interest and participate at any level from being an observer to being an influencer or thought leader of such groups. In addition, individuals can use social media and collaborate primarily by communicating with friends and associates and secondarily to self-brand and self-market.

Technology has opened up the capability for socializing on a global scale for everyone. Virtually no one is restricted or confined from digital access. The social media presence is growing beyond the traditional grandfather of social media—Facebook. Just about every ethnic, age, educational, and other demographic group has a presence on or access to Facebook, Google, Nings, YouTube, blogs, talk radio, and tweeting. The point is, social media, in this context, is about communities of individuals who have come together, joined by a variety of digital communications channels (for example, Facebook, LinkedIn, Twitter, Digg, Meetup, Google+) bound by a shared interest or purpose. This is what makes social media different from anything man has done up to this point.

The second group consists of entrepreneurs, businesses, and organizations that use social media to collaborate with their markets and stakeholders. This is transparent communications of social media, interpersonal relationship building, branding, lead generation advertising, promotion, and marketing.

Starting with the technology, it is apparent that America is embracing social media in a big way. Based upon the broadband usage and numerous studies of Internet usage, it is fairly certain that at least 77 percent of the population have regular access to the Internet, and about 68 percent of people with an Internet connection use social media in some form.

The value of social media is found in the productive collaboration of multiple communities, on a massive scale, simultaneously and productively leveraging the knowledge, experience, backgrounds, thoughts, intuitions, research, and ideas of any people on a variety of issues, problems, opportunities, and solutions. The wisdom of the crowd, the benefits of the diversity of heterogeneous thinking, all add to the value of a vast network expanding the value chain.

Social media enables you to connect with, collaborate, and follow up with colleagues of similar interests nearly instantaneously and without geographic constrictions; this capability provides an enormous advantage over traditional face-to-face networking. However, the same advantages are the roots of social media's disadvantages. The ease of just building large communities, regardless of their location, tends to make these connections less permanent, less cohesive, and less desirable as effective tools of reciprocity.

The social media revolution is being driven by the Millennial Generation, those 81 million hip young people born between 1977 and 1998 who author Don Tapscot called the "first net generation." The seduction of social media is the temptation to try out all the new social media gimmicks, tactics, ideas, concepts, and technology just because they are available and everybody is on board because it's cool and hip.

Another temptation is to repeat the Internet error—to use the vast potential of the medium to oversell and then underperform—by trying to overwhelm as many people as possible with technological cleverness and cuteness and then litter the space with spam, junk offers, and other clutter.

Because the social media train has supposedly left the station, individuals and businesses may feel technologically backward if they haven't kept up. Individuals may feel handicapped if they don't have hundreds of Facebook friends or a Twitter site or several Google+ circles, whereas businesses and organizations may feel as though they must have a social media presence or be "out of it" in the eyes of their customers and prospects. This approach is like the "ready, aim, shoot" mentality of the early days of Internet marketing.

We should have learned the lessons of the dot-com mistakes, but sometimes it helps to be reminded of what went wrong with the killer app of the World Wide Web. Peter Drucker, one of the great business thought leaders of the twentieth century and author of the first book on the profession of management in 1954, proposed three questions that were classic inquiries into strategic thinking:

1. What is your business?

2. What will be your business?

3. What should be your business?

The questions were seductively subtle, and often senior executives were put off guard by their steamily simplistic substance and missed the important issue Drucker was trying to get them to see. For any individual thinking about employing social media effectively, it would be wise to rethink and paraphrase Drucker's three questions:

1. What is your social media strategy?

2. What will be your social media strategy?

3. What should be your social media strategy?

In the early 2000s, there was no social media as we think of it today. Therefore, there was no need for a social media strategy per se. However, every individual, for his or her personal use, and every chief executive, president, owner, operating officer, or executive director has the responsibility, regardless of the time—be it pre-social media, pre-Internet, pre-technological revolution, today, or in the future—to work daily on visionary and strategic thinking, in addition to the time spent on actual tactics and implementing the items of the social media menu, about the future of his or her social media activities or businesses.

Social Networking and Employment

There has to be a better reason to become social media literate than just to be considered hip. One aspect of social media that needs to be reinforced, by awareness and skill training, is the proven success of strategically applying it to personal networking and job hunting. A great deal of research has clearly demonstrated the benefits of personal networking (referred to previously in this book as the "informal" job hunting approach) as the most effective tool for job searching and career advancement available to individuals.

Remember to exercise *caution* **when using social networking.** Potential and current employers are viewing social networking activities and content. Be aware of the information you are sharing on these sites, as well as your e-mail address. Select a professional email address and refrain from using nicknames or sexy connotations in your e-mail address.

As you consider the strategy of using social media to support your job search or career enhancement, one critical point must be front and center: An enormous amount of data out there demonstrates employers are looking for *good people* who can adapt to change and meet the ever-changing needs of business. Employers want skills and characteristics that, for the most part, are transferable from recent graduates from formal education to military veterans.

Job seekers are going to have to be adroit at demonstrating their ability to translate their personal skills, abilities, characteristics, and background experiences into the skills that employers need now and in the future. You don't want to possess these skills and abilities and throw away their value by not displaying them well.

A significant amount of research and writing has been done in this area, and Michael is currently involved in conducting another major survey on how the supply side—the employers—view, perceive, and use networking. The early results of this research confirm the data from dozens of previous studies, which show that employers want and need "good people" but generally have trouble finding them.

This data says the formal methods of job search, including digital postings, job fairs, resumes posted on employer Web sites, recruiters, classified ads, cattle calls, mass mailings of resumes, cover letters, and even what we teach in our educational system, are not working very well. This is demonstrated in the literature. Instead, as the data indicates, there is more likelihood that the job search will be successful if job candidates use the informal methods of personal networking and direct application to the hiring manager as their major tools. Of course, this is not to say they should not use other tools—they should—but as part of the job search repertory, this approach is situational and conditional depending on each candidate and job search.

Potential employers and even schools have a tendency to search social Web sites before they interview candidates for jobs and entrance into higher education. Also, current employers randomly check Web sites after hiring you. Content is creating a first impression, and first impressions are always powerful, so make yours memorable. Social networking may be the source of your initial contact with your next employer.

Digital Communications Last Forever!

Use your knowledge to be empowered about what your social presence is saying about yourself. If you have any doubt about whether you should or should not post specific information on a social site, *don't* post it; follow your instincts. If your instincts don't lead to proper decision making, check with a trusted professional to determine the appropriateness of what you would like to post on the social sites.

Using social content properly can highlight your knowledge of and proficiency with technology. Your level of professionalism, displayed through technology and networking, connects you to the business world. Networking professional sites such as LinkedIn can show your association with businesses, which can be beneficial by creating collaborations.

Social Media Isn't for Everyone

Not every individual will adapt social media into his or her life. For some people, as you will see, social media is not applicable for them; others are just not ready to accept the benefits and value of social media. **Misuse of social media can lead to many unpleasant results from something as a simple embarrassment to a major public relations nightmare to even legal action.** Social media is not suitable when deep analysis of a topic is required, when information is required by certain intermediaries or experts, when certain safeguards or security standards are required, or when sharing with large groups is inappropriate. Regardless, social media is a phenomenon that is having an extraordinary impact on individuals and businesses; therefore, it should be understood.

Is Social Networking for You?

Although social media use has grown dramatically across all age groups, older users have been especially enthusiastic about embracing new networking tools. All you need to do is watch the growing number of TV ads for the "mature" Internet matching and dating services to see the growing acceptance among baby boomers and silent generation types regarding how social media can meet their needs.

Although e-mail continues to be the primary way older users maintain contact with friends, families, and colleagues, many users now rely on social network platforms to help manage their daily communications—sharing links, photos, videos, news, and status updates with a growing network of contacts.

Half (47 percent) of Internet users ages 50–64 and one in four (26 percent) users ages 65 and older now use social networking sites. Half of online adults ages 50–64 and one in four wired seniors now count themselves among the Facebooking and LinkedIn masses. That's up from just 25 percent of online adults ages 50–64 and 13 percent of those ages 65 and older who reported social networking use in a survey conducted in April 2009.

Young adult Internet users ages 18–29 continue to be the heaviest users of social networking sites such as Facebook and LinkedIn, with 86 percent saying they use the sites. However, their growth has paled in comparison with the gains made by older users. Between April 2009 and May 2010, Internet users ages 50–64 who said they use a social networking site such as MySpace, Facebook, or LinkedIn grew 88 percent, and those ages 65 and older grew 100 percent in their adoption of the sites, compared with a growth rate of 13 percent for those ages 18–29.

Summary

Many people your age probably have viewed networking as something primarily more mature people do, perhaps a cultural icon of the baby boom generation. However, if you look at the subject more closely, networking is the common thread of all successful people, regardless of their age, profession, field, or endeavor.

Now the digital generation—you—have a networking tool that you grew up with, are comfortable with, and are linked to by your usage and skill set. That tool is digital communications. It is not a replacement for traditional face-to-face networking skills, but an enhancement. If it is used properly, you have the opportunity to develop into far better networkers than previous generations.

In the next chapter, "Organizing and Keeping Track of Your Network," you will learn how to arrange a simple but effective database to keep your networking organized.

10

Organizing and Keeping Track
of Your Network

By Stephen L. Faulkner

Don't expect this chapter to be full of high-tech jargon and recommendations for state-of-the-art computer hardware and software. The theory here is that you should use the KISS system, or you won't keep any system at all. The KISS system is Keep It Simple, Stupid (said lovingly, of course). A system will work if you use index cards or a database system such as ACT!, Excel, Lotus Notes, GoldMine, or any other computerized database.

Whatever system you choose, from sticky notes to the latest computerized database system, it needs to be easy to use and simple to access; otherwise, you will not use it consistently. Your system should work for you; you should not have to work for your system. The master networkers live by this axiom. The information they need is always at hand because their system is organized and accessible. Take time to set up your own system and then make sure to keep it up-to-date.

You need to take the step of setting up a contact database. Many people have started with one approach and through trial and error moved on to other systems. The important point to remember is *build something that works for you.* Here are a few tips to help you get started:

1. Enter contact information: name, title, company/school, address, phone number (cell, land line), fax number, e-mail address, and URL if appropriate.

2. Enter each contact's preferred method of communication.

3. Enter "details" you want to remember for your contacts, such as personal interests, books they like, clubs they have joined, sports they enjoy or play, foods they like, their majors in school, their hobbies and interests, arts and entertainment interests, music and bands they like, family information, organizations to which they belong, their job information, and birthday and holiday information. Include any information that will help you make better connections.

4. Use A, B, C prioritizing (see "Keeping in Touch with Everyone in Your Growing Network" in Chapter 7, "Keeping Your Network Alive and Growing").

5. Keep a history of contacts and conversations with each person.

6. Include the best time and place to contact each person.

Networking

The key to keeping your network organized is to maintain an easy-to-use database of contact information. In the old days, that may have meant index cards stored in a box. In the 1990s, networking meant you could throw out the index cards for an Excel spreadsheet. The ability to organize and keep your network with you at all times has hit a milestone with the invention and proliferation of smartphones.

The future only makes networking easier.

Notecards

Initially, I used notecards when I was looking for my first job—not because I didn't have access to a computer, but because it was easier for me to jot down the information after meeting someone or having an interview.

My system involved writing the name, company, position, and contact information on the card, along with all the times I reached out to each contact. This system has its flaws in that sometimes poor handwriting can make index cards illegible. Then you run the risk of accidently throwing them out.

> Pros: Easy to set up, inexpensive

> Cons: No backup, difficult to maintain, easy to lose or misplace

Steps to Success:

> Develop a pattern for filling out, organizing, and storing cards and stick to it.

> Ensure you include name, address, and how to contact person.

> Make room to jot down other pieces of information such as contact history, next steps, personal notes, and so on.

> Write legibly.

Excel/Spreadsheets

With a box full of incongruent note cards, I soon realized the importance of good penmanship and organization. So I switched to an Excel-based method. Adding contact information into an Excel sheet allowed me to keep everything organized and enabled me to create mail merges with word processing software, so I could create cover letters customized to go along with my resume. This approach cut the need to write out these letters by hand and allowed me to send more without developing carpal tunnel syndrome.

The pitfalls of using only Excel are common with any other computerized system. You should make sure to save your files and remember where they are stored. Files can easily be lost if you have a sloppy naming system. When doing a mail merge, you should still proofread your finished document—as I found out when one of my fields (the company name) was somehow not updating. I sent out several resumes to people with a cover letter detailing my interest at working for a company that was not their own.

Excel is currently the easiest way to set up and keep a networking database organized.

> Pros: Easy to customize, integration for mail merge

> Cons: Resides only on the computer

Steps to Success:

> Set up a spreadsheet in Excel to include name, address, and other contact information.

> Add fields to include notes, contact history, or other important information (interests, hobbies, family information, and so on).

> Save the file in a folder or on your desktop to make it easy to find.

> Save the file regularly.

> Use Word or other word processing software to set up a mail merge for letters or envelope labels.

Google Docs

Google Docs revolutionized the ability to seamlessly collaborate with people on a single document. It also allows you to create a contact database and save it online for you to access anywhere. Google Docs can work on PCs, Macs, smartphones, and tablets, letting you create a free and easy way to keep track of your network.

> Pros: Portability, accessible with any computer

> Cons: Learning curve if new to Google Docs

Steps to Success:

> Create a Google account.
>
> Follow the same advice as for using the Excel spreadsheet.
>
> Google Docs also allows you to perform mail merges. Integration into Gmail also allows you to send out personalized e-mails.
>
> Google Docs automatically saves each change you make.
>
> If you make a mistake, Google Docs keeps track of your revisions and allows you to revert to a previous version.

Apps

Believe it or not, smartphone apps can do more than sling birds across your screen. More than a thousand apps on both the Android and iOS platforms allow you to set up an address book, keep records of contacts, and share information with other users. Picking the right app is a matter of choice; it can come from either the free selections or the paid apps.

> Pros: Extreme portability, plenty of selection
>
> Cons: Lack of backup, could cost money

Apps are too different to provide basic guidelines for, so instead, here are **Summary Steps to Success for Keeping Your Networking Database:**

> Develop a pattern for filling out, organizing, and storing cards—and stick to it.
>
> Ensure you include their name, address, and how to contact them.
>
> Make room to jot down other pieces of information like contact history, next steps, personal notes, etc.
>
> Write legibly.

The Future

By the time you read this, the "future" may already be here, so take this section with a grain of salt. The future of networking will be even easier than having an app on your phone. After people get past the initial privacy concerns about Google Glasses, this invention could revolution-ize how you develop and interact with your network. Imagine being able to pull up information about a contact simply by looking at that person. The same way you now cannot find your way without GPS, with Google Glasses, you may never need to remember a name again. This capability could allow you to share information by just talking to someone.

Summary

No matter how you choose to organize your database of network con-tacts and information, the important point is to have a system and stick to it. A key to successful networking is follow-up. Having a well-organized and up-to-date database, and a system to access it, will help you do this.

In the next chapter, "Getting Up to the Door for the Interview," you will learn how to put all the elements of networking together to help get you to the interview—then it's up to you.

11

Getting Up to the Door for the Interview

If you expected the "five secrets to acing the interview," this chapter isn't the place. Just remember that networking—no matter how good you get at it—will not likely get you the job. Networking can get you up to the door; networking can move you up in a long line of applicants; networking can help you get noticed; networking can shorten the time of the job hunt; networking can improve your chances of seeing the right decision maker; networking can position you in the best light; networking can do a lot for you, including getting you up to the door for the interview in the best possible light. Then it's all up to you and your skills.

There is a great deal of data (both research and anecdotal) available regarding the conditions of the job market, along with types and availability of positions, job seekers, and workers. There is also a fairly large volume of information that specifically examines the extensive use of social connections—networking—in obtaining information about the job market, potential jobs, and the actual recruitment and hiring of candidates. The data shows that the most successful methods employed for finding out job information and acting on that information are the *informal* methods of networking and direct application to the company in contrast to the *formal* methods of job placement firms, classified ads, recruiters, agencies, government job assistance bureaus, and other traditional methods.

Even as the growth of social media has provided you with a widening array of digital communications choices to enhance social networking, there is still one constant despite a world moving at a dizzying pace of modernization and technological and social change. The greatest potential for assisting in a job search depends on how much you are embedded in your social networks: your relatives, friends, and acquaintances.

Using Your Networking Support System

Networking, as a social support system made up of people you know and trust and whom you believe you can depend on, will influence your success in life and society, your sense of well-being, and even your health. The overall importance of your networks cannot be exaggerated. It is through personal contacts that society is structured and you are integrated into society. Although modern nations have elaborate arrays of institutions and organizations, daily life proceeds for individuals through personal ties: In many occupations, workers recruit family members and friends; parents choose their children's doctors on the basis of personal recommendations; people select foods, restaurants, and vacation spots on the advice of friends; and investments are made on the advice of tennis and golf partners. There are endless examples, but the point is the same. The interactions among individuals and parts of society are the same; they turn on the personal dealings between individuals who know one another and are part of a personal network.

Because you will spend so much of your life in your job and career, the networking affecting this part of your life is extremely vital.

In any decision situation you face, there is one common problem: You face the decision without having perfect information. The future is unknown, and in a job search, you simply do not, nor will you ever, have complete information about either the job or the employer. From the job provider's perspective, the process of researching candidates through the traditional formal job search methods is not rational because this is simply not an efficient use of time or resources. The long-term success of candidates hired after using traditional methods is not better than candidates hired through networking methods.

Labor economists, sociologists, academicians, and laypersons have known for a long time that many job seekers hear about and obtain their jobs through their friends and relatives. This approach is less costly in time and money than virtually any other and may be more productive than most in terms of generating better job offers.

Building relations can pay off in jobs, leads, sales, partnerships, mates, friends, ideas, and ways you have not even thought of yet. The key is to establish a relationship before you need it. Here are some tips in doing so:

1. **Understand the goal.** Darcy Rezac in his book, *The Frog and Prince: Secrets of Positive Networking to Change Your Life* (Frog & Prince Networking Corp, 2003), wrote what we think is the world's best definition of networking: "Discovering what you can do for someone else." Herein lies 80 percent of the battle: Great networkers want to know what they can do for other people, not what others can do for them. If you understand this, the rest is just mechanics. Wolves know how to sniff out what others need, and wolves are uncanny about finding ways to help fill those needs.

2. **Get out.** Networking is an analog, contact sport. You can't do it alone, and you cannot do it just from your home, office, on the phone, or via a computer. You may hate them, but force yourself to go to trade shows, conventions, and seminars. It's unlikely that you'll be closing a big order with someone you met online at

MySpace or via Skype. Get out there and in person, face to face. Wolves network; sheep hide in their offices.

3. **Ask good questions; then shut up.** The mark of a good conversationalist is not that you can talk a lot. The idea is to get others to talk a lot. Thus, good networkers are good listeners, not good talkers. People love to talk about themselves but do not like to be grilled. A question such as "What do you do?" may seem like an innocent opener, but it could be too direct and probing.

   How about something like "this seems like an interesting group of people; do you all work in the same field?" and that can lead to "Oh, how did you get into that field?" "Where are you from?" and "What brings you to this event?" are also follow-ups that create open-ended opportunities. Just listen. Ironically, you'll be remembered as an interesting and also a smart person. Wolves ask and listen; sheep just listen.

4. **Unveil your nonbusiness passions.** Talking only about business is boring. Good networkers unveil their passions after they get to know you. Great networkers lead off with their passions. Your passions make you an interesting person, so spend time talking about them. Wolves have a voracious appetite for the things they love and will seek out opportunities to share this passion and hear others share their passion. Sheep are happy to huddle together and say, "'blah blah blah' or 'bah bah bah.'"

5. **Read, Read, Read, Read.** To be a good networker (and listener), you need to read a lot. You need a broad base of knowledge so that you can access a vast array of information during conversations. Even if you are a boring person, you can at least be a well-read one who can talk about a variety of topics. Wolves want to know as much about everything as possible, so they read journals, newspapers, trade magazines, online content, and books, and they go to seminars and conferences. Sheep want to huddle quietly in front of the TV and count people.

6. **Follow up.** Why would people bother asking for a business card if they're not going to follow up? Great networkers follow up within 24 hours. Just a short e-mail will do: "Nice to meet you. I hope we can do something together. Hope your blog is doing

well. I loved your Breitling watch. I have two tickets to the Stanley Cup Finals if you want to attend." Include at least one thing to show the recipient that he or she isn't getting a canned e-mail.

7. **Make it easy to get in touch.** Many people who want to be great networkers, ironically, don't make it easy to get in touch with them. They don't carry business cards, or their business cards don't have phone numbers and e-mail addresses. Even if they provide this information, it's in six-point type. This is great if you're schmoozing teenagers, but if you want old, rich, famous, and powerful people to call or e-mail, you'd better use a 12-point font. Wolves leave tracks and a scent, and they hunt for contacts. Sheep mill around, and if they make a contact by accident, that's great. But they have no plan and put in no effort to build the network; that would mean they'd need to follow up, and that is too much work.

8. **Do favors for people.** One thing that can give you a lot of pleasure in life is helping other people without the expectation of return from the recipient. Reciprocity is the expectation that once a favor is given, one will be returned to you—even if you don't expect it or ask for it. Doing favors for others can be its own reward, but we get an extra measure of satisfaction when that person acknowledges our thoughtfulness and returns a favor to us. This exchange of favors is a step in the building of a stronger networking relationship. Mentors often bestow gifts and favors on those they mentor because they want to show the younger person they have a true interest in their well-being.

Summary

Lots of people are "qualified" for the jobs and career positions that you want (and deserve). Some people may be more qualified, some just as qualified, and some less qualified. How organizations sort out candidates for positions can be a Byzantine, complex, bizarre, unfathomable, bafflegab of unknown processes and operations. In the end, the best person doesn't always get the position for many reasons.

Networking is the most effective tool for job seeking and career development because it keeps these functions more in the control of the individual than traditional job hunting and career development techniques. If you feel that you deserve an opportunity, then using networking to leverage yourself into a position to demonstrate your skills and abilities over others not only makes sense but also proves you have stronger management and leadership skills. Isn't this what organizations are looking for? Of course.

In the final chapter, you will look at plans, commitments, and successes of some people like you who have used nonstop networking techniques to achieve their goals and dreams in life. Chapter 12 will tie together all that you have examined so that you can begin to build your own network and gain the benefits.

12

Tying It All Together

We are always delighted when we get a text message, the phone rings, or we get an e-mail, and a contact informs us that we were right, these techniques really do work, and the person wants to share his or her story with us. We hear stories all the time about new job offers, exciting new career opportunities, fantastic business ventures, wonderful new relationships, or just accounts of newfound confidence or personal development in meeting people and making connections. The letters and messages we receive in which people have said that their lives have been transformed because they have made networking a part of their daily existence are the most gratifying of all.

Now we hope that you too are benefiting, or will benefit, from the principles, tools, rules, ideas, and techniques of nonstop networking. You can incorporate every single thing we have described in each chapter—from attitude and techniques to continuity and organization—into your daily life starting NOW!

- **Attitude:** Networking is a lifelong process.

- **Techniques:** You have all the techniques at hand to make it happen.

- **People:** Every contact you make is the chance to learn something new.

- **Organization:** Keeping contacts and information at your fingertips is easy and rewarding.

Attitude Is Everything

When you started this journey, you saw how a negative attitude could stop you from networking—how negative attitudes actually do stop people from networking.

This was the case with the students in a UCLA survey who, by an overwhelming margin, saw that networking was successful but couldn't bring them to do what it took to be successful. Yet, when you give yourself permission to network and change from a negative to a positive outlook, good things begin to happen. It really is in your hands and mind.

You will find a common theme among these and other stories of successful networkers: The harder they work, the luckier they seem to be. Go figure.

Some names and details in some of the following examples have been altered to protect the privacy of all parties involved.

The Photographer's Story

Andreas's friend, the photographer, asked, "What do you mean the opposite of networking is *not* working?" That did not make sense to her. It seemed to her that networking is not only work; it is hard work! What Andrea meant was that when you are not networking, you are simply not working. You are just standing still in life, like the photographer who was afraid to get out there and network, get clients, and start her own business.

The photographer then followed the steps in this book. Here's her story in her own words:

"I took baby steps. I planned what to say when I met new people. I developed a thirty-second infomercial about myself. I went through my old address books and reconnected with old friends and colleagues. The more I did, the better I became at these skills.

"Actually, it wasn't as though I was not good at it in the first place. I liked meeting people. It was just that I had a bad attitude about 'networking.'

"What happened was an epiphany of sorts. I stopped thinking about myself and networking for my business and focused on the people I was meeting and reconnecting with. As Andrea suggested, I looked for ways to be a resource and to make connections. I love to entertain, so I put together a series of dinner parties where I concentrated on putting together people I thought would enjoy meeting one another. I also hosted a number of neighborhood get-togethers. I recall remarking to my husband after one such event, 'We are so fortunate to have so many interesting neighbors, from all walks of life.'

"My network expanded as I continued to meet people and reconnect with those I had lost touch with. I was having fun! And my business got off the ground. My thirty-second infomercial was effective—I think mostly because I am so enthusiastic about my new profession. Also, everyone has something to say about photography, and almost everyone needs a portrait of themselves or a family member, a pet, or even a house.

"I see now what Andrea means when she says that every single person we meet is someone we have an opportunity to learn from. Everyone has something to offer, and who knows, that person may turn out to be a potential client for you. My business is still young, but all of the clients I have so far have come from networking efforts. The amazing thing is I don't think of it as networking. It is just meeting people and talking about something I love to do."

Armed with Your Arsenal

You have all the techniques at hand to make your goals happen. You can use them at any event or in any situation that arises. To use them effectively, just remember the following:

- Know who you are.
- Focus on the needs of others.
- Have a goal.
- Work at it.

Know who you are. How do you want people to remember you? Is it more than just your business card? Is it a comment or remark you make that causes someone to say, "Oh really? How do you know that?" Is it the description of you delivered with natural enthusiasm and, yes, even with passion?

Focus on the needs of others. Keep your conversation starters and get-to-know-you questions fresh and timely and focused on the other person's needs. Practice your openers and watch how your conversations become easier and more interesting. Your goal is to get others talking about themselves so that you can learn their needs and how you can be a resource to them.

Have a goal. Networking is a lifelong process; however, your networking goals will change throughout your life. At any given time, you may be more or less concerned with the following:

- Finding a job
- Getting a promotion
- Looking for a career change
- Finding a life partner
- Looking for a new business venture
- Looking for new business clients
- Examining your political aspirations
- Reevaluating your personal interests
- Looking for a lifestyle change
- Moving to a new location
- Getting on interesting assignments and the best project teams

Keep working; never quit. Networking is a lifelong journey that will bring a lifetime of rewards to those who keep working at it. Armed with the techniques in this book, you can accomplish your goals in these or any areas of your life.

John's Story

"The most important thing I was introduced to in college and the thing that was stressed the most by Dr. Faulkner was the importance of networking. From reading Andrea's first book on networking and

Dr. Faulkner's lectures, I started to take a different approach to the way I did a lot of things. I took a different approach on how I usually present myself when meeting people for the first time. One major thing I have learned is the importance of understanding body language and the effect it has on networking and the perceptions of others. People form perceptions of you before even meeting and getting to know you.

"The real test came when the college career services department put me in touch with a company called Berry Plastics. The firm wanted a copy of my resume. With Dr. Faulkner's help, I created a resume that was achievement oriented and one that focused on the kind of skills and character traits businesses want in new college graduates.

"The initial interview led to others, and I built a network of contacts with each person with whom I met. When I was hired by Berry Plastics, several departments requested that I be assigned to them.

"The biggest changes in my resume from other templates and styles I had been presented with previously was that I included and highlighted the accomplishments I had achieved at different jobs instead of the standard job description items. I wound up getting the job I wanted. I think a good part had to do with changing my resume around using the networking skills, including writing a follow-up handwritten thank-you note to everyone who interviewed me.

"After getting the internship at such a large facility with over 300 employees, I was able to start to put networking skills I have learned to work. From working in different areas of the company, I started to meet all different types of people, from people with different levels of authority to people of different races and age groups. Before I knew it, I had gotten to know at least fifty people with whom I felt I had made a good impression. In the future, if I need anything, I feel like I could ask any of them for a favor.

"One thing I also did was watch how I presented myself at all times, making sure to project good body language even if someone did something that annoyed me such as not getting me some type of information I needed at a certain time. By creating a positive image with all of the management in the company, anytime they would introduce me to someone, such as an auditor or higher level of authority, they would say something good about me. This allowed me to meet and get to know lots of people with respectable positions because of how I networked with the right people to make a positive image of myself in their minds.

"This is what brought me to my current contact, which is the vice president of business and financial planning for the company. I got to meet him because my company has an annual meeting where three top people, one of whom is the vice president, come for an all-day meeting to go over the financials of the company. Throughout the meeting, a lot of management had good things to say about me and how I helped them out and was a good person. After hearing all of this, the vice president found me to introduce himself and talk to me about staying with the company because of the great things people said about me, which all started by networking.

"Right now I am in a training stage to get to know more about the company and to see if this is the career path I would like to take. They are willing to create a position for me and are having the financial manager of half the company come out from Chicago to spend time with me. All of this started through networking."

Deborah's Story

Andrea's friend Deborah, a vice president of an advertising agency, told of how she found her life partner by setting a goal and using networking techniques.

First, Deborah wrote out exactly what she was looking for in a life partner. For starters, he had to be a certain age and religion, and he had to come from a background similar to hers. He had to have many of the same interests as her, including a zest for travel. Most importantly, she was looking for someone who shared her values and goals, especially about raising a family.

Next, she identified the places where she would likely meet such a person. She joined specific business and social interest groups, she got more involved in her church, and she taught a course at a local community college. She joined a board of a local nonprofit group and volunteered to chair an event. She also began networking at her health club. Deborah was just living her life, but adding a networking component. She joined and got involved with things that interested her, but with the specific goal of making contact, knowing that one of these contacts might turn out to be, or lead to, her life partner.

She also, however, subtly told others about her goal. In business terms, she asked for referrals. Ultimately, that is how she met Doug, whom she later married.

Along the way, she met many interesting people, dated several prospective life partners, made some beneficial business connections, and found some lifelong friends.

She says she also fine-tuned networking techniques, which have served her well in a subsequent job search.

Identify and Expand

Every contact you meet is the chance to learn something new. Keep identifying these people and the places they gather. Build on your current database of contacts and seek out new ones. These contacts enrich your life and lead you to relationships that help you achieve your life's goals.

Tom's Networking Plan for a Public Relations Agency

Andrea's friend and publicist, Tom, successfully incorporated a networking plan into his business plan. This has helped him stay on track to expand his network and grow his business. Tom says the following about his networking experiences:

"Before I opened a new office in downtown Chicago for my growing public relations firm, I wrote a business plan that included a networking strategy. I had been working with Andrea for a number of years, and she had not only taught me the techniques of networking, but I knew from firsthand observation of the growth of her business that they worked.

"Since a key aspect of public relations is building relationships with the media, the first thing I did was find a location close to the offices of every major national and local media outlet in Chicago. I did this for convenience and visibility for my firm.

"Then, after attending a couple of meetings and meeting some people, I joined two key networking organizations: the Chicagoland Chamber of Commerce and the Central Michigan Avenue Association. Both of these organizations provided opportunities to network with businesses that need to get their names in the media.

"At the beginning of each month, I make a special networking plan. I look at three important areas from which to choose my networking activities: what organization events and meetings I can attend, what upcoming meetings and conventions listed in the business press would be worthwhile, and lastly which TV or radio producer or reporter contacts of mine I should arrange to meet this month. I make calls, mark dates on my calendar, and follow up.

"The meetings I set up with my media contacts are in addition to ones where I am pitching a particular client or story. I simply try to learn more about my contact and his or her publication. This strategy makes it easier to connect when I do want to pitch a client or story. While most of the time these meetings are just for gathering information and staying in touch, sometimes they lead to bigger opportunities.

"One time while I was having lunch with the editor of a national business publication, he asked me if I could recommend someone for a panel on business-to-business Internet marketing. I helped him out by introducing him to a contact of mine who was a marketing manager for a national wireless phone company. It was a networking win for me for two reasons: First, I became a resource for the editor, and second, it gave me a reason to reconnect with my contact at the wireless phone company, so I could keep my name in front of him. Subsequently, I've had the opportunity to meet with him to discuss future business.

"Another part of my networking plan involves day-to-day contacts. I learned from Andrea's advice to network everywhere, even in your elevator. For example, when I am in the elevator on the way up to my office and the other person is getting off at a different floor, I sometimes say, 'Hi, may I ask what you do on floor...?' So far, I have made connections with a graphics design agency and a national investment firm. I just keep identifying and expanding my contacts, and my business keeps on growing."

Organize It All with a Kiss

Develop a simple system for keeping your contact information readily available.

Connecting with just four people a week puts you ahead of most people who claim they are networking. Recall our "FOUR-mula for Success" from Chapter 6, "How to Expand Your Network"? Every week just call, e-mail, text, or write a note to

1. A client, customer, or prospect (remember, we're all in some kind of selling).

2. A former colleague or coworker.

3. A former classmate or friend.

4. A current classmate or friend.

The process could not be simpler!

Melissa's Story

"When I was introduced to the idea of networking, I thought it had to have something to do with computer gadgets. Was I ever wrong in that impression. What my professor, Dr. Faulkner, was referring to was social networking, or better yet, professional networking and building contacts to help us change our lives.

"We were being introduced in class to this idea that we could impact our job hunt, career development, and personal lives by developing a network of people who would be willing to help us if we were willing to help them. We were taught in class to build our personal networks with people we already knew and then continue building it with people we would meet along the way.

"Networking involves communications with people on a mutually agreeable time schedule and finding ways to help each other. The simplest and quickest way I used to build up my network was by membership in the online social network sites of LinkedIn and Facebook. I built a profile of myself, which included information about school, past and present professions, interests, and other topics. These memberships allowed me to be connected to more people from school, work, and those with the same interests and goals in life. For those who I knew or came in contact with who could not connect with me online, I keep a hard copy address book plus a computer database of addresses.

"I have had some great experiences with networking. For example, my first job out of college was in the medical education field, and I got the initial interview through my friendship with a college staffer who was a friend of the hiring manager of the company that hired me. It was one interview followed by a job offer on the spot.

"The position I held for two years put me in touch with many highly regarded individuals who became speakers for our company. I developed a large network from this and helped a number of these individuals manage career moves and secure high-level speaking opportunities, in addition to other favors I obtained for them. As a result, many people in my network have returned or sought to return favors to me. I have been contacted for a number of positions without ever having to apply, I have been invited to appear in commercials and as an extra in a movie, and I get called by well-known speaker bureaus and asked to help them fill in open speaking slots. These are just a few of the benefits I have gotten back from my willingness to help others. Networking, in my eyes, is a big key to succeeding in almost anything in life."

It's a Forever Process, and It Isn't Easy

We (Andrea and Michael) have both had this experience: Former seminar participants, students, friends, family members, business associates, even colleagues have approached us and said, "I tried networking once, tried for three or four months, and I stopped because nothing happened. I didn't get the job I wanted, didn't meet whom I wanted. It was too hard, and it didn't work for the amount of effort it took."

To these people, we say, "What did you expect to happen in three or four months?"

Networking is about building relationships, which takes lots of time and lots of work.

There is no timetable, no schedule for success. There are no quick and easy formulas, no shortcuts. Networking is hard work, and the people who are dedicated to the techniques will be successful; those who are not dedicated will not be successful. It's that simple.

Kristine's Story

"College students often doubt the power of networking. We grow up listening to that old tried-and-true statement: 'It's not what you know, it's who you know,' and after hearing this time and time again, we begin to doubt the importance of networking.

"However, once graduation day rolls around, college students begin to realize that there is nothing but truth to that statement.

"As a college student myself at DeVry University in North Brunswick, New Jersey, I have learned the importance of networking in college firsthand. College is nothing like high school. You need to treat every class, every workshop, and every opportunity as a potential connection to your future. Rolling out of bed, wearing your pajamas to school, and keeping to yourself is no longer an option. That amazing paper you write and leave on your professor's desk could lead you to a desk at the corporate office you have been dreaming about since you signed those acceptance papers. How? It's because of networking.

"Perhaps the professor who read your paper knew someone who worked at your 'dream corporation.' Since you were involved on campus, and made a good impression, you were first on his or her recommendation list for that interview. Now you have your foot in the door at your dream job and can continue to network and climb the corporate ladder.

"While enrolled in college, I became heavily involved with various activities and clubs on campus, produced A+ work, and showed that I was willing to go above and beyond what was expected. I was polite to every guest on campus, paid attention to those who my mentors and professors knew, and made it a point to obtain employment on campus. As a result of my networking efforts, I was voted valedictorian of both my associate's degree–level class and my bachelor's degree–level class by DeVry faculty. I also had the opportunity to serve as an officer for many clubs on campus and be nominated as a student representative. As a result of my on-campus presence, I now have many leads for future employment opportunities."

Like Kristine, your college success revolves around recognizing the importance of networking and taking full advantage of it. There is always someone in a college setting who shares your same interests, is willing to listen to your ideas, and/or can offer helpful information. Additionally, if that individual cannot help you, then nine times out of ten, he or she can connect you to someone who will, thus proving the importance of networking.

Networking by Necessity

You might be right to think that finding a job should be effortless when you have a well-crafted resume that shows your years of experience. This is probably true in theory. In practice, however, the hiring process in Turkey works completely different. Sometimes, some candidates could be luckier than others because of their contacts in power. In other words, influential relations can open the doors to candidates unquestioningly. That could cause some unfair circumstances for the people who deserve the most attention.

Of course, the hiring practices in Turkey are probably no different from those in most parts of the world. Because family ties are strong in Turkey, job applicants who are relatives of current workers have a strong advantage over nonrelated applicants. Although company size is important in the evaluation process, the main objective of a job applicant is to have a powerful network and be known either as relative or know someone powerful in the company. If there is no candidate for an opening within the network, the hiring process works through the formal process; that is, the job is advertised, applications are taken, and applicants are interviewed, and those candidates who are most qualified are selected.

Most of the companies in Turkey are run by families. Personal biases are significant in the hiring process. Companies that are public or governmental have established human resource departments with traditional hiring processes. Additionally, government jobs are seen as lifetime guarantees in the workplace. Hiring in government employment is done through a multiple-choice centralized exam, which is held every two years.

The following story, then, highlights how Evrim learned the value of networking.

Evrim's Story*

"I had emigrated from Turkey and at the time knew no one in America. I was searched and applied online for a job and was thinking if I don't know anyone for reference, nobody will call me back; however, I was wrong. Networking is very important for that kind of job in 99% of the cases; another 1% is depends on your luck and experience. I believe in that mine was falling on that 1%. This networking statement has been proved after I got my job.

"If you know someone inside that can be reference for you make it can be easier to get the interview but not getting the job, this you have to be able to do on your own. For you to get the job is depends on how you present yourself with your professional appearance and behavior during the interview. If you can answer all the questions within the way the company expects which is focused on customer orientation, ethical behavior, and respect for fellow employees, peers, and coworker.

"When the phone rang and they asked if I was still interested in for the position that I applied for Chase Bank.... My heart was pounding!!! I said, "Yes, I am still interested in." The hiring manager was very kind and set up an interview. However, this was for another location and part-time teller position. I still accepted that interview. I was also working at Macy's at that moment.

"All I wanted was to step into a position in one of the biggest financial company in the country and I wouldn't have any reason to return to a part-time job at Macy's. It would be the first step to enter the business world without any reference.

"I accepted the offer even though it was part time and I know I might be staying in part-time role without any time frame. I didn't even think twice 'offer accepted!!!'

---

* Author's Note: Evrim was born in Turkey and did not learn to speak English until after she immigrated to America less than a decade ago.

"That's how my Chase Bank journey started but not ended... After 4 months they offered me full time and then my hard work started to open all dream doors I wouldn't even imagine. I was just one of that hard worker single mom to make things happen for her son. It is just not the life harder; it is also what we are making it harder. Now, I can proudly say I am part of the management team for the company that gives chance to make your dream happen. My journey started almost 5 years ago as a part-time teller and continued Assistant Branch Manager within 2 years. I still love what I do as an ABM and seek to expand my network with meetings, events, and individual contacts with people."

It's Your Choice

Now is the opportunity to choose—the decision time. As stated in the beginning of this book, nearly everyone has the opportunity to choose the pathway to his or her future success, a pathway to success or mediocrity. Many people will never be aware that they have this opportunity and therefore will never choose. The fortunate ones become aware of this opportunity and choose success; others are aware and choose not to put forth the lifelong effort. The decision pathways are fundamentally a crossroads.

One pathway involves following along and basically handing over your future to whatever you believe life has to offer you. That can be whatever life hands you, whether it is fate, cosmic forces, the flock mentality, randomness, luck, predestination, good decisions, or a combination of these and other things mostly out of your control.

The other pathway involves choosing networking as a life-altering technique and tool and then beginning—and never stopping—to use the technique and tool to choose your life options. Will you still face obstacles, setbacks, job losses, failure, heartbreak, defeat, uncertainty, roadblocks, randomness, bad luck? Possibly. Many of us do. But you can manage your setbacks better, and they should have a less detrimental impact on your life because you will have the safety net of your network. We cannot predict the future, but if you encounter any or all of these difficulties, you will have techniques and tools to help you face them and realign yourself toward your new goals and objectives. Furthermore, you can have the techniques and tools to use your network of contacts that will help you achieve more, learn more, do more, be more than you could otherwise.

Many will want to decide to make networking part of their lives, fewer will actually start, and more will drop away because of the commitment to hard work required. However, the dedicated ones (the wolves) will continue on, and they will more likely be successful in achieving their goals and objectives in life. At the end of the race, the others will be on the outside looking in, wondering why they didn't get better jobs, wondering why they didn't get more or better promotions, wondering why they didn't get more plum assignments, wondering why they didn't get to meet interesting people and do more interesting things, wondering why they got less out of life than they expected and wanted. Those on the inside looking out will know the answer....

The future is in your hands—you have the choice.

A

Five Steps to Networking

Step 1: Meet people.

Step 2: Listen and learn.

Step 3: Make connections.

Step 4: Follow up.

Step 5: Stay in touch.

B

Fourteen Easy-to-Use Techniques for When "It's Time to Network"

1. Have a business card.

2. Have an "ice breaker" opening line.

3. Develop your 20- to 30-second "branding statement." Some people call this an "elevator statement" because you should be able to complete it on a short elevator ride. This infomercial about yourself provides the listener with a reason to pay attention to you.

4. Do your research; know something about your potential network associates.

5. Have a list of "get to know you" questions prepared and practiced so you sound natural.

6. Develop a list of idea generator topics ("small talk").

7. Get in line.

8. Take a deep breath; visualize yourself engaged in a thoughtful, interesting, and memorable conversation; and dive into a group.

9. Look for a designated host or greeter, and start there.

10. If you and the contact have your hands free (no juggling of plates and glasses), extend your hand first and offer a firm (but not bone-crushing or limp) handshake and introduce yourself. Be sure to consciously talk slower than you normally would because your adrenalin is pumping and you'll be talking faster than you think.

11. If you are seated at a table, start a conversation with the person to your right or left.

12. Have an exit strategy, a "break the contact" comment that allows you both to break off conversation gracefully.

13. Set a goal for every event or activity you attend to build your network by some number.

14. Follow up with a thank-you.

C

The Networking Process

We like to think of the networking process as something you can **post** on your bulletin board or on a mirror as a constant reminder:

P = Create a **Plan** that fits your **P**ersonality.

O = **O**wn it in an **Organized** fashion.

S = **S**tick to your own **System**.

T = **T**ake **Time** to build relationships.

D

The Five Action Steps of Building and Growing Your Network

---

1. Identify the people who can help you.

2. Compare this list to the list you started in Chapter 3—those people you know will take your call.

3. Reconnect with those already in your network and keep up the contact as your network grows.

4. Identify the organizations and activities where people you want to know gather.

5. Get involved in these organizations.

E

Make F.A.C.E. Work
for Your Networking

F = Make it **Fun**. **Find** unique things to do and places to meet.

A = **Adapt** to each other's timetables and surroundings.

C = **Connect** and find common interests.

E = Know when to **Exit**; be respectful of each other's time.

Sources

Cornell University Career Services. "Networking Events." http://www.career.cornell.edu/events/networking/.

Faulkner, M. 2009. My polls. LinkedIn. http://polls.linkedin.com/. Accessed June 30, 2010.

Forrester NACTAS, Q2. 2006. Youth, Media, and Marketing and Financial Online Survey. Cambridge, MA: Forester Research.

Gallup. 2009. Strengths-based development: Using strengths to accelerate performance. http://www.gallup.com/consulting/61/Strengths-Development.aspx. Accessed January 10, 2013.

Gray, C. F., and E. W. Larson. 2008. *Project Management: The Management Process*. 4th ed. New York: McGraw-Hill/Irwin.

Hart, P. December 2006. *How should colleges prepare students to succeed in today's global economy?* Washington DC: Association of American Colleges and Universities.

Nierenberg, A. 2002. *Nonstop Networking*. Sterling, VA: Capital Books.

Putnam, Robert. 2000. *Bowling Alone: The Collapse and Revival of American Community*. New York: Simon & Schuster.

Index

Numbers

2-2-2 strategy, 88

A

action steps for building and growing
  your network,161
active listening, 63
activities
  etiquette, 106-108
  identifying where people you want
    to know gather, 81-861
adjusting to personality styles of
  others, 50-51
anniversaries, 95
appreciation
  characteristics of great networkers,
    51-52
  e-mail, 99
  gifts, 99-100
  handwritten notes, 95-96
  holiday greetings, 97
  "The Power of Three" note plan, 98
  sending notes, 97
  thank-you notes, 96-97
apps, organizing your network, 131
articles, writing, 89-90
asking for favors, etiquette, 113-114
asking questions, 136
association, 84
attending events, 69-70
attitude, 140
photographer's story, 140-141
audiences, social media, 119
auditory learners, 49

B

baby steps, 66-67
become a resource for others, 101
become active, organizations, 88-89
become known, 89-90
behavior, social media, 119
birthdates, 95
body language, 27
branding statements, 30-32, 157
breaking the ice, 27-30
building relationships, 135-137
business cards, 27, 107, 137
Business Network International
  (BNI), 82
business space, 107

C

candidates, researching, 135
caring, characteristics of great
  networkers, 56-57
cellphones, etiquette, 108
characteristics managers are looking
  for, 9-11
characteristics of great networkers,
  45-46
  appreciation, 51-52
  caring, 56-57
  confidence, 46-48
  empathy, 48-51
  enthusiasm and energy, 55-56
  rapport building, 57-58
  tenacity, 52-55
chemistry, 29, 101
committees, joining, 88-89